NANNYING:
A GUIDE TO GOOD PRACTICE

Please retu...
...r or ...

Christine Hobart • Jill Frankel

Text © Christine Hobart and Jill Frankel 2001
Original illustrations © Nelson Thornes Ltd 2001

Published in 2001 by:
Nelson Thornes Ltd
Delta Place
27 Bath Road
CHELTENHAM
GL53 7TH
United Kingdom

01 02 03 04 05 / 10 9 8 7 6 5 4 3 2 1

A catalogue record for this book is available from the British Library

ISBN 0 7487 4501 7

Illustrations by Ian Heard

Page make-up by Columns Design Ltd

Printed and bound in Great Britain by T.J. International

CONTENTS

ABOUT THE AUTHORS

The authors come from a background of nursery teaching and health visiting, and have worked together for many years training students to work with young children. They have written ten books that encompass the childcare and education curriculum.

ACKNOWLEDGEMENTS

The authors would like to thank the Professional Association of Nursery Nurses (PANN) for their help and support, and for permission to use the contract of employment on pages 189–92, and to Leslie Frankel for taking some of the photographs. The publisher would like to thank Associated Press Limited for permission to use the photograph on page 166.

FOREWORD

The Professional Association of Nursery Nurses (PANN) has no hesitation in endorsing a book which gives good, sound advice to nannies, the most vulnerable group of the childcare profession.

The nannies we meet are always hungry for advice, support and for furthering their childcare knowledge and expertise. They long for the recognition and professional status enjoyed by all other childcarers but which is often sadly missing in their employment.

Many employers do not wish to issue contracts, intend to pay their nanny cash in hand and see no value in ensuring that adequate insurance cover is in place to protect the nanny and the child/ren in her care.

PANN would urge all nannies to become familiar with their employment rights so that from day one they can look forward to a trouble-free and long-time career in what many one-time nannies describe as the 'best time of their lives'.

Tricia Pritchard
Professional Officer, Professional Association of Nursery Nurses and Chairman, Playpen, The Campaign for Nanny Registration and the Regulation of Nanny Agencies

PANN can be contacted at: 2 St James Court, Friar Gate, Derby DE1 1BT (telephone 01332 372337).

INTRODUCTION

This book is written for people who are either working as nannies or wish to make a career of working with families. This is possibly one of the most responsible jobs in childcare, and experience and training are both important. A nanny, either residential or non-residential, provides stability, consistency and reliability of care and increasing numbers of parents are finding this a satisfactory option.

The aim of this book is to reinforce what good nannying should be. Throughout the book we have emphasised the importance of mutual respect and confidentiality and how vital it is to obtain a contract of employment and a job description before undertaking any employment, so that there are clear expectations on both sides.

There are many features that should prove helpful: case studies, activities, good practice, charts that can be copied and used and lists of further reading and useful contacts. The text describes safe and up-to-date practice that meets the children's needs in all areas. We have devoted some chapters to job hunting and confidence in interviews. At the end of the book, you will find advice on financial and employment issues, and how to live in harmony with the family you choose.

Throughout the book, we use certain conventions. The nanny is referred to in the feminine gender as the vast majority of nannies are women. After tossing a coin, the child is also referred to in the feminine gender.

1 NANNYING AS A CAREER

This chapter includes:
- Why people employ nannies
- Why women work
- Different types of nannying
- Why people work as nannies
- Training and experience
- Registration

Being in sole charge of children is one of the most challenging jobs there is. Ask any mother! When the children are not your own, the responsibility for their development, safety, care and learning is even greater.

It has been estimated that there are approximately 110,000 nannies working in the UK. A recent survey commissioned by *Nursery World* found that nannies care for an average of two children, most of whom are up to 3 years of age, and that a nanny usually stays with a family for just over a year. Being a nanny is the only form of childcare and education employment where qualifications and registration are not compulsory. This can make a nanny very vulnerable and anyone working as a nanny must have a contract of employment and hold personal liability insurance. Belonging to an organisation such as PANN (the Professional Association of Nursery Nurses) is recommended as it will provide essential information and support should you need it.

Because being a nanny is so demanding, and because most parents expect so much from their nannies, training and qualifications are very important. Training will allow a nanny to gain an understanding of the total needs of the child. It will also give her confidence in her own ability and status.

Why people employ nannies

There could be several reasons why families consider employing a nanny. The mother may be returning to work after maternity leave. It could be that a parent is left on his or her own to cope with the children, and decides to employ a nanny so that he or she can work to support the family. A mother may be going back to a career after caring for her children full-time during the early years. She may have decided to try working from home and needs someone to look after the children while she concentrates on her work. Indeed, some mothers may not be planning to work at all, but feel the time has come to find someone to help with caring for their children, particularly if they have a large family. There are many advantages and disadvantages of employing a nanny in the home rather than using other types of care.

ADVANTAGES OF EMPLOYING A NANNY

- The child will be less disturbed by change.
- The child can build good relationship with her carer.
- The child has her own toys and equipment to play with.
- The child has her own carer to nurse her when she is unwell.
- The child will be able to visit extended family members during the day.
- The child can attend special leisure or activity classes chosen by the parents.
- Siblings can remain together.
- Working arrangements can be flexible to suit parents.
- Parents can choose the child's diet, patterns of rest, exercise and sleep, and her friends.
- Parents can decide how qualified and experienced the nanny needs to be.
- The nanny can accompany the family on holiday, so that the parents can have more time for themselves.

DISADVANTAGES OF EMPLOYING A NANNY

- There is no official check or registration of nannies with the local authority.
- The nanny may not have training, qualifications or experience.
- A nanny is more expensive than a full-time private nursery, if there is just one child in the family.
- The parents will have to take responsibility for financial and insurance matters.
- The nanny may become isolated.
- There will be wear and tear on the house.
- There is no supervision of the nanny during the day, or evidence of what goes on in the house when the parents leave for work.
- If living in, the nanny may bring her personal problems with her into the home.

Why women work

Many women today wish to combine careers with bringing up children. Some women are leaving it later to start a family, and are usually quite well established in their careers. They are able to afford to pay for help with the children. Younger women, perhaps not so advanced in their careers, often feel that it is worth making other sacrifices, such as giving up holidays and going out to the cinema or a restaurant, in order to pay for help so as to continue to climb the career ladder.

Increasing numbers of women are returning to work following childbirth. Research shows that two-thirds of mothers resume their careers within eleven months of having a baby and that they are returning to work sooner after giving birth. Within 28 weeks of having a baby, 81 per cent of women go back to work and, of these, 20,000 women a year in the UK return to work after less than 14 weeks maternity leave. For many it is a financial necessity to maintain their standard of living, while for others it is important not to interrupt their careers for too long a period. Some employers operate schemes to help women employees to balance work and family commitments by providing opportunities for flexible working hours, job shares, dependency leave, and workplace nurseries. These are in the minority, and most mothers will return to employment, with no acknowledgement of their new responsibilities or help with childcare from their employer.

Some people find it difficult to understand why mothers are willing to leave their children in the care of other people. Many parents feel a sense of loss when they return to work. They miss their children and feel guilty at leaving them. Stereotypes in the media of women who 'want it all' are not helpful. It is important to respect the decision of mothers to return to work, even if their children are very young.

Different types of nannying

Nannies work in a wide range of family settings. For example a nanny could:
- live in with the family (residential)
- work a set number of hours a day, while living elsewhere
- work with two families
- work abroad
- work in the town or work in the country
- work full time or part time
- work as a temporary nanny
- work as a maternity nurse with newborn babies in their first weeks of life.

In one job, you might be expected to provide full care for the children of the family, and take sole responsibility while the parents work, and in another you might work in partnership with a parent who is always at home. Occasionally, two families will combine resources to employ a nanny. You might particularly enjoy working with newborn babies, and specialise as a maternity nurse who works with a family for a number of weeks and has special responsibility for the newborn baby. You may work with a family and live in their home or you can be employed on a non-residential basis.

You would find working in the country very different from a job in the city. Working abroad should be avoided until you have gained some experience. It might suit you to work part time if you have family commitments of your own. You may prefer not to spend all your time with one family, and enjoy the challenge of temporary work, often filling in while the family nanny is on holiday.

RESIDENTIAL WORK

Advantages of residential work
There are many advantages to residential work, such as:
- no daily journey to work
- the possibility of travel with the family
- money goes further – no rent or fares to find
- no food bills
- the possibility of better communication and contact with the parents
- living conditions are usually good
- the possibility of an enhanced lifestyle
- not having to worry about finding comfortable accommodation.

Disadvantages of residential work
However, there could be many disadvantages, such as:
- lack of privacy
- being asked to do more than you should, for example being expected to babysit without prior notice
- feeling guilty if unwell
- being expected to work, even if you are unwell

- accommodation being tied to the employment
- not being treated as part of the family
- being caught up in the emotional problems of the family
- not being allowed to entertain friends
- feeling isolated from your peers
- the line between private and professional life becoming blurred, as children do not understand the concept of being 'off duty'.

NON-RESIDENTIAL WORK

Advantages of non-residential work

There are advantages to non-residential work, such as:
- having control of your own social life
- clearly defined hours of work, therefore you are less available to be taken advantage of
- ability to change jobs more easily, as you have your own home base
- being perceived more as a professional person
- parents being prepared for you to bring your own child to work. These days, having a baby need not be the end of your nannying career.

Disadvantages of non-residential work

There are, of course, also disadvantages to non-residential work, such as:
- money not going as far
- having to allow for travelling time, with perhaps a difficult journey to work
- greater difficulty in communication and liaison with parents
- parents not always getting home on time, thus disrupting your plans
- having your own accommodation, which can limit your job choices.

CASE STUDY

Jane, a recently qualified eighteen-year-old nanny, accepted a job as a live-in nanny in Kensington. The mother interviewed her at the agency offering the job, so Jane had not seen where she would be living. When she arrived at the house she was overwhelmed at the size and grandeur of the home. She realised that the lifestyle of the parents would be similar to those she had seen only on the television. She felt somewhat dismayed and apprehensive.

1   How could Jane have been better prepared for the job?
2   How might Jane ask the parents to make it clear what was expected of her?
3   How would Jane find out about any support systems?

After qualifying as a childcare and education practitioner, working in a private family can offer useful and valuable experience. It can be a comfortable and exhilarating life and, although you may feel isolated from your professional peer group from time to time, it is important to keep in touch with current ideas and good practice.

It is sensible to work in the UK, gaining experience and skills, before seeking work abroad. Certain countries are seen to be more dangerous to women on their own than others, so do seek advice from your union or from the agency that is offering you the job.

Try to learn the language and the customs of the country and remember that there are many different customs, traditions and even games that will differ from those with which you are familiar.

If wishing to work outside the European Community, it is a good idea to get in touch with the embassy of the country concerned and find out what documentation is needed. It is intended in the European Community that all professional and educational qualifications will eventually become acceptable in any member state, so it should become increasingly straightforward to obtain work in Europe.

Make sure that wherever you go, you have enlisted the aid of a reputable agency, and that you have sufficient money for emergencies and a return flight.

TEMPORARY WORK

You would need to be very flexible to enjoy this type of work. Temporary nannies are usually employed in emergencies, such as when:
- families are suddenly temporarily between nannies
- parents have to go away unexpectedly
- parents go away on business trips, or take a holiday
- one parent is ill, and the other has to work
- covering short-term while the family finds the right permanent nanny.

Because of the nature of the work, you would need to be very well-qualified, confident in your practice, and able to establish routines with all age groups. You will need to be assertive as it is likely you will need to collect information from the parents very quickly before they leave you in sole charge. This work would suit only the most experienced person.

NANNY SHARE

Families who wish to defray costs and provide company for an only child might consider a nanny share, where the families share the costs and administration of employing a nanny. If you were offered this opportunity, it is important for you and for both families to be clear on issues such as:
- child-rearing
- diet and food preparation and provision
- suitable activities for all the children
- arrangements for the families to share
- insurance requirements
- responsibilities such as tax and national insurance
- arrangements for sharing homes
- having suitable toys and equipment in each house
- arrangements for holidays
- a contract of employment from both families

Childrens' games may be unfamiliar to a new nanny working in another country

- the length of the arrangement and how to cope with the sudden withdrawal of the children of one of the families, thus losing part of your salary
- age of children (small babies may be too close in age for you to give appropriate care)
- travel arrangements between homes.

Most nanny shares work out well, once all the pitfalls have been discussed and resolved. You need to be highly organised and there should be regular meetings between you and both families. It is often a good idea to use one home for a certain length of time, say a week, and then use the other home. A formal written contract between the two families will sort out the issues. Local branches of the National Childbirth Trust (Head Office telephone number: 020 8992 8637) often hold Nanny Share Registers, so it may be worth contacting them if you are considering this type of job. If more than two families share a nanny, you will need to be registered by the local authority as a childminder.

CASE STUDY

Melanie was asked by her employer if she would consider caring for her friend's baby as well as the toddler and young baby she was already looking after. It meant a rise in salary, so Melanie agreed. After a week she realised she had made a mistake, as it was impossible to give both babies the attention they needed, and the toddler who was already jealous of his own brother became bewildered and confused, and was obviously upset by the situation.

1 Should Melanie have agreed so readily to take on both babies?
2 What should Melanie say to the parents?
3 How might she help the toddler?
4 If the situation continues, what might the long-term effects be on all three children?

Why people work as nannies

Many people qualify as childcare and education practitioners in order to work as nannies, as they see it as a way of becoming independent and leaving home. Being part of a team in an establishment does not appeal to everyone. They prefer the challenge of organising their own work and using their initiative to care for children in a family setting.

The vast majority of nannies are female. Most men prefer to work in establishments where there are career prospects and some families would not consider having a male nanny.

There are many advantages to being a nanny. You may be:
■ working in a safe comfortable environment, with a pleasant family, and with perhaps the opportunity for travel
■ working in a close relationship with a small number of children
■ making decisions and using your own initiative
■ able to socialise with other nannies
■ given opportunities to meet a variety of different people through the parents
■ experiencing a different lifestyle or culture.
There can be disadvantages, such as:
■ the possibility of feeling isolated
■ parents possibly not understanding your role
■ conflicts over child-rearing practice, conditions of service, or job description, with the parents
■ no training or career development prospects.

Activity
Can you add anything to these lists? What, for you, would be the most important advantage?

If you have decided that you want to work as a nanny, you need to:
■ think carefully about the sort of family you wish to work for
■ prepare yourself thoroughly for any interview, remembering to ask questions yourself
■ make sure you spend time with the children and the family before making your decision. If you are not sure, ask for another visit
■ be sure you do not agree to work for someone with whom you feel uncomfortable
■ agree a written job description, contract and conditions of employment
■ spend as long as you can with your employer, finding out all the routines, likes and dislikes before being left in sole charge. Find out whether your ways of managing the children's behaviour are similar to those of the family
■ demonstrate your respect, appreciation and trust in your employer
■ always be aware that the parents are the most important people in a child's life and work with them in partnership.

Training and experience

Training for work with young children comes in many different forms and at many different levels.

The fact that you have committed yourself and completed a course of study shows a serious interest in working with children and may indicate to the family that you will stay longer and have a professional commitment to them. You will have learnt about childcare and education, child health and development, and should be very familiar with the needs of babies and young children. A qualified person with experience is most suited to be in sole charge of small children. Most qualified nannies do not expect to take on any duties other than those related to the child. For example, you would only be expected to clean the children's rooms, make the children's meals, and wash and iron the children's clothes and would not do this for other members of the family.

Some families prefer to employ qualified nannies who have had experience with different families in various situations. If you have experience as well as a good qualification you will have much more choice of jobs, as employers will be able to check references, acknowledge your experience with different age groups and appreciate the commitment you have shown to each family. On the other hand, newly qualified nannies are much in demand, as some families might feel threatened by a person with a great deal of experience, and prefer a younger nanny.

Registration

At the moment there is no recognised registration system for nannies although several high-profile child abuse cases involving nannies and au pairs have given this issue some impetus in the past few years. It has been realised that starting up a registration scheme is not as straightforward as was once thought.

- The costs of setting up and administration would be expensive.
- It might give parents a false sense of security, and they would not complete their own checks.
- Who would be expected to register – should it include mothers' helps and au pairs or be limited to those with a professional qualification?
- What checks should be asked for? It would not be possible to ask for medical records for ethical reasons, and yet an employer would not want a nanny with mental health problems.
- Being on a register will not show up a child abuser unless there has been a conviction.
- Being on a register does not, of itself, raise standards.

A national register would reassure parents, and provide police checks. It might engender some basic training requirement. It would give a local authority a better idea of the total childcare and education provision in the area. It would give nannies the same status as other childcare and education workers.

Several voluntary registers and organisations have been set up, such as the National Accredited Nanny Association (NANA) of PO Box 24, Uckfield, East Sussex TN22 4ZX (telephone: 01825 732666). NANA confirms you are who you say you are, checks your CV and qualifications before issuing you with a photo card. This demonstrates to employers that you have nothing to hide and that these checks have been done. There is a charge for this, and the card needs to be updated regularly.

There is no doubt that if you want a career as a nanny, and you want it to be rewarding and successful, the route you take in looking for the perfect job and interviewing really well will be a crucial part in your success.

2 *FINDING YOUR FAMILY*

> ## This chapter includes:
> ■ **Job search**
> ■ **Preparing for an interview**
> ■ **The interview**
> ■ **Making a decision**
> ■ **The contract**
> ■ **The job description**

Having decided that you wish to be employed as a nanny, the process of finding employment can be long and demanding, so it is as well to start looking in good time. If you are on a course which finishes in July, May would not be too early to start the process. The more time and effort that you put into finding the right job, the more chance there is of a successful outcome.

Job search

The main ways of finding a job would be to go to an employment agency in your area, by word of mouth, or to look in specialist magazines, such as *Nursery World* or *The Lady*. Sometimes advertisements are carried in daily or local papers or seen on a college notice board. As you become more experienced and known in the neighbourhood, you may be recommended to a family. For a newly qualified nanny, the safest approach is obviously through an agency, as they should have interviewed the prospective family.

AGENCIES

According to PANN, only 30 per cent of nannies are hired through agencies. Anyone can register with a private employment agency to look for work. There are many that specialise in childcare employment, offering both permanent and temporary vacancies. The agency may put you in touch with a prospective employer, or may employ you themselves to work in a variety of different settings.

Agencies will require information from you relating to your qualifications, past experiences, skills, and personal details, and will request names of referees. Reputable agencies will take all reasonable steps to ensure that nannies are suitable for working with children. They will offer the parents copies of at least two references. They are not allowed by law to charge a fee to the job seeker. It is the employer who pays the agency for filling the post.

The Recruitment and Employment Federation of 36 Mortimer Street, London W1 (telephone: 020 7323 4300) produce a directory of childcare agencies. They requires their members to abide by a code of good recruitment practice. The members have to:

- ask candidates to complete a detailed application form, outlining personal details, qualifications, experience and employment history. Agencies and families will always wish to see original documents, so show them the originals, but take copies to leave with them
- ask candidates to state whether they have a criminal record
- check the identity of the candidate, by examining a document such as a birth certificate, driving licence or passport
- explore fully gaps in employment history
- check original certificates of qualification
- interview all candidates in person
- take up at least two references to confirm competence and suitability.

When all these checks have been carried out successfully, the agency will then proceed to the next stage, introducing candidates to families where they appear to be suited by experience, qualifications and personality. Agencies should provide full and relevant information to both parties before an interview while respecting the confidentiality of both. They should never offer misleading information or advertise wonderful sounding jobs that do not exist.

The government is planning to introduce a voluntary code of practice for agencies. The agencies that take this up will be recognised by a kite mark, which would reassure parents who are looking for a nanny. PANN believes that the code of practice should be statutory, to ensure that all agencies work responsibly.

Before registering with an agency, check that:

- they have vacancies in the area of work that meets your needs
- they have a procedure for vetting prospective employers
- they will assist you in negotiating terms and conditions of employment and in the drawing up of a contract
- after placement, support is offered by the agency if there are problems.

ANSWERING INDIVIDUAL ADVERTISEMENTS

If you apply through a paper or a postcard in a newsagent or on a college notice board, you should be aware that there are risks involved. If you set up an interview in this way, you should at the very least let someone know where you are going and who you are going to see. It is safer still to take someone with you. In this situation there is anxiety on both sides, as parents may be reluctant to have someone waiting in another room while they interview a prospective nanny, so your friend should be prepared to wait outside the house.

If the interview is to take place in a hotel, insist that it is carried out in the reception area, where there are plenty of other people around. Never agree to be interviewed in a hotel bedroom or private room on your own.

CASE STUDY

Tracey replied to an advertisement in her local paper for a post as Nanny to two children working abroad. The money was good, and the conditions of employment sounded excellent. She was invited to attend an interview at a nearby hotel.

When she arrived she was sent up to a room, where two men were waiting. It became clear that interviewing for a nanny was not the first thing on their minds. Fortunately, she realised this quickly, and managed to leave the room without further involvement, but felt shaken and distressed by the experience.

1 What steps should she have taken to protect herself before the interview?
2 What steps should she have taken to protect herself during the interview?
3 What steps should she take after this experience?

After your first job, it is quite likely that you will hear of other posts through personal contacts and recommendations, and this will do a great deal to offset any fears you may have in approaching new families.

PROFESSIONAL JOURNALS AND NEWSPAPERS

You will find nanny jobs advertised in professional journals, magazines, and in local papers. These may also carry a risk and care should be taken to protect yourself.

The papers and journals will carry advertisements for a wide range of different childcare employment. A good advertisement will tell you about the family, the job itself, and something of the qualities of the applicant required by the employer.

You may be asked to respond in different ways:

- by making telephone contact
- sending a handwritten letter of application
- sending a simple letter requesting details of the post
- sending a curriculum vitae (CV).

It is important that you respond as requested in the advertisement.

Activity

Look at four different copies of *Nursery World*. List four nanny jobs in order of preference. Why do you prefer these jobs?

JOB HUNTING TECHNIQUES

It is useful to keep a record of your job applications (see page 16), keeping track of what post you have applied for, the date of application, interview date and the response. It is helpful to try and assess why you were successful, or not, and if the job for which you had applied was right for you. This information will be useful in future job applications.

Always keep documentation in a secure place, retaining copies of the application form, the advertisement, and any information sent to you by the family, so that you may refer to it before the interview. It is likely you will apply for a number of posts as you finish your training, and keeping a childcare job search record will help you to be clear about the progress of each application. If you are not offered employment, the reasons why may emerge from this record, particularly in your comments.

Applying for any employment requires careful planning, preparation and organisation. You will need to understand the stages and sequence of the application process, and approach it with the same enthusiasm and professional skills as you do in all your work.

PREPARING YOUR CURRICULUM VITAE (CV)

Curriculum vitae is a Latin phrase meaning 'the course (or story) of your life'. It has come to mean that area of your life that you have spent in employment, and an outline of other experiences and interests that may be regarded as relevant by a potential employer.

If you have access to a word processor, you will find it easier to tailor your CV to each specific job for which you are applying. While being totally honest, you should emphasise the particular strengths and experiences required by the post. Remember that you may well be asked to elaborate on any area of your CV at interview.

Nanny job search record				
	1	**2**	**3**	**4**
Where advertised: date				
Employer: Name Address Telephone				
Ages of children				
Full-time/part-time/nanny share				
Residential/non-residential				
Type of response requested				
All details received: date				
Application made: date				
Interview: date				
Outcome: date				
Comments				

Points to remember

The CV should be typed, and presented tidily on white A4 paper. Some people think that an imaginative and unusual presentation will have more impact. It may, but it could put as many people off as interest others. Ask friends, colleagues or tutors for their response.

- Spelling and grammar must be correct. (Have it checked.)
- Keep it brief. It should be no more than two pages long.
- Avoid solid blocks of script.
- Use space to emphasise points and make sections stand out.
- Get a tutor or friend to check it for any ambiguity. It may be clear to you but muddled to an outsider.
- Update it regularly.
  Your basic CV should include:
- personal details
- education and qualifications
- work experience and career history
- personal interests and hobbies
- other relevant details
- names of referees.

TELEPHONE TECHNIQUE

You may be asked in an advertisement to make telephone contact with a named person. Give yourself time when doing this and make sure you are not going to be interrupted. Try to use a private phone rather than a pay phone, and have the advertisement by you when you ring. Speak slowly and clearly, stating where you saw the advertisement, your reason for interest in the job, and your name and full address, including the post code. The telephone conversation might turn into a short-listing interview, so make sure that you have your CV with you, so that you can answer any questions clearly and concisely as to your qualifications and previous experience. You may wish to make some notes yourself, so have a pencil and some paper available.

Preparing for an interview

This stage of obtaining work is possibly the most nerve wracking and worrying part of finding a job. You feel at your most exposed and vulnerable. Being well-prepared will help you to become confident and so succeed.

When you have been given an appointment for an interview as a nanny, you need to check that you are clear about the time and date of the interview, and have the correct address.

- If you live fairly near, it is a good idea to make a trial journey, so as to find out exactly where it is, and how long it will take you to get there.
- If you have to cancel your appointment let the family know immediately.

- Let a friend or relative know where you are going, and at what time. You have to be careful. You may ask a friend to accompany you to the house or place of interview, and wait outside until you are ready to leave.
- Look neat, clean and tidy. Decide what you are going to wear in advance, and choose clothes that are neither extremely smart, nor extremely casual. You want to look relaxed and comfortable and able to cope with small children, avoiding too much make-up and jewellery.
- Gather together your CV, any open references or testimonials and certificates of training and education to take with you to show to the family.
- If you have recently qualified, take your college and placement reports with you. Some employers might like to see some of your college assignments and files.
- You may be asked for proof of identity, so take with you your passport, driving licence or birth certificate.
- Try to anticipate and prepare answers to questions you may be asked.
- Prepare some questions of your own.
- Ensure that you arrive in good time, but not too early.

The interview

In most instances, this will take place in the informal home setting, with just one person, or at most two. The children may well be around, and most parents would be anxious to note the interaction between you and the children, so even though you may be nervous, make sure you do not ignore any member of the family.

When talking to the parents, make sure you are sitting comfortably, removing any heavy outer wear, and feeling as relaxed as possible. Listen carefully to what you are being asked, and answer appropriately, neither too briefly nor in a rambling manner. Take your time to consider each question put to you, and answer honestly and positively. If you find you are being asked questions that only require one-word answers, take the initiative yourself, and extend the answers. If you think most of the questions you are being asked are either irrelevant or too personal, after a while say so clearly and calmly, being assertive but not aggressive. Try not to be put off if notes are being taken or recordings being made; they will be used only to help the person remember your good clear answers, particularly if he or she has several people to interview.

Most interviews will contain some of the following questions.

- Do you have any childcare qualifications?
- What is your past childcare experience?
- Can you supply at least two references that can be followed up?
- What interests you about this particular job?
- Are you in good health? Are you receiving any medication or therapy?
- How long do you see yourself working for this family?
- What are your views on: play and stimulation, food and mealtimes, social and educational activities, toilet training, ways of discipline, rest, exercise and sleep?
- In what ways will you maintain a safe environment?
- How would you plan a daily routine for the children?
- How would you cope with difficult behaviour, for example, if one of the children said they hated you or, in a temper tantrum, bit another child?

- Are you familiar with this area and local childcare facilities?
- Do you drive?
- Do you smoke?
- Have you a past record of drink or drug abuse?
- Have you any objection to household pets?
- Would your religious or political views make it difficult for you to work in this household?
- If not living in, how would you travel here punctually every day?
- Do you have any special dietary needs?
- Is this job likely to conflict with other responsibilities in your life?

After a thorough discussion of the children's needs and your ability to fulfil these, you may be offered the job. Disappointments often occur on both sides because certain difficult issues have not been adequately discussed, and people enter into a contract with different expectations. Therefore it would be sensible for you at interview to be clear about the following.

- How much housework will be required of you? (A trained nanny should be expected to take on chores related to the children and the children's rooms and washing only, whereas a mother's help by definition would take on a wider range of duties.)
- Who will provide which meals, and where will you eat?
- Will you have access to a car?
- What access will you have to a telephone?
- Will your male and female friends be allowed to visit you in the house?
- Have you discussed the family's views on television watching, fast/junk food, outings?
- Will you be expected to look after other children from time to time?
- What accommodation will you be given (if the job is residential)?
- How often will you be expected to babysit, and will you be paid extra for this?
- When will you be given a contract of employment?
- What arrangements will be made for payment of salary and deduction of tax and national insurance?
- Is adequate insurance held by the employer?
- Does the employer have a procedure for administering medication to the children and seeking medical advice in an emergency?
- Will you be expected to keep a daily diary to share with the parents?
- Who else is living in the house?

You may not wish to ask all these questions, and some of the answers may well have come about during your general discussion. There might be other things you wish to know, which are particularly important to you. It is worthwhile spending quite some time at the interview, as each family is unique, and you want to make quite sure that you will fit in well. Try to be totally honest as if you are caught out being economic with the truth it may be a cause for dismissal and may damage your future career.

Most importantly, trust your instincts. You will know right away if you feel on the same wavelength as the family, and if you like the children. Do not feel you have to accept the first job offered to you, take your time, and remember all interviews are valuable experiences.

BODY LANGUAGE

Your appearance and speech will tell the family a great deal about you. Your body language will also convey messages. What you say should fit with your body language, otherwise the employer will be very confused and perhaps not believe what you are saying.

Remember:

- When you enter the room, put your belongings away from you, stand up straight, walk slowly into the room to help you stay calm, and use a firm, not limp handshake.
- Make yourself comfortable as you sit down. Sit back in the chair, and try to relax.
- Look pleasant, but do not grin inanely.
- Do not be over-familiar with the interviewers. Address them by the names they have given you.
- Make eye contact when responding to a question.
- Do not put your hand across your mouth.
- If your hands are shaking, keep them out of sight, and do not accept a drink.
- Listen intently to any questions, showing respect to the interviewer.

Making a decision

If you feel the job is right for you, it is prudent not to accept it immediately. Make an appointment for a second interview when you can meet other members of the family, and watch the children playing together. Most employers will be happy to do this, as they can see how you interact with the children, and gain the opinion of further family members.

You may be offered the job subject to references and a medical examination. Well done! Make sure you have enough information with which to form an opinion, as to whether or not you wish to accept the post. You need to consider:

- whether the offer is conditional. If so, on what?
- the starting date
- the salary and subsequent increments
- the travelling time and cost if you will not be living with family
- whether there is a probationary period
- whether the conditions of service, appertaining to hours of work, holidays and sickness arrangements are fair and satisfactory
- whether you felt comfortable with the people and the atmosphere in the house
- whether the job will use your skills and talents enough to stretch you, and give you job satisfaction.

Even after two interviews you can still say no, and you should be prepared to do so if you are not sure about some aspect of the job that is important to you. For example, it might sound wonderful in every respect, but you cannot agree with the parents' ideas and opinions on disciplining their children. Some nannies might say 'yes' out of desperation, thinking they will never find the perfect post.

It is important to be confident and realise your value. There are more people looking for professional nannies than nannies seeking jobs. Discussion always helps. Your agency or a close friend will be happy to talk it through with you. It is sometimes useful to write down everything you think will be good about this job, and some areas you feel may be not so positive.

If you are already working do not hand in your notice until you have received the offer of the post in writing. If you are not offered the job, try not to be too disappointed. There are several steps you can take.

- Write down the details of the interview, the questions you were asked, how you responded, and if you were satisfied with your response. Recording what happened may well help you with your next interview.
- Ask for feedback, why were you not appointed? It may take courage to do this, but it might be helpful for the next occasion.
- Read about how to be an effective interviewee.

Do not take failure too personally; there may have been much better qualified or more experienced candidates. Sometimes there is so little to choose between the best two or three applicants for a job that it is little more than luck at the end. Keep going!

The contract

When you have come to a decision, you must request a contract. If this is agreed in advance it will prevent many ambiguities and ensure that both parties have the same expectations of the role. Employers are obliged by law to give an employee a written contract of employment after eight weeks. A contract should include by law:

- date of issue
- name and address of employer
- name and address of employee
- starting date of employment and period of employment (if appropriate)
- place of work
- salary
- details of deductions for national insurance and income tax
- hours and time of work, plus any babysitting arrangements
- confidentiality clause
- sickness arrangements. If you are ill and living in, is there any cover for you? What are the arrangements for sickness pay? Who will look after you?
- holiday arrangements
- insurance
- probationary period and probation arrangements
- period of notice to terminate the employment, required by both sides
- any pension arrangements
- disciplinary procedures
- duties and responsibilities and job description (on a separate sheet). See Appendix, PANN Nanny Contract of Employment (page 189).

It was Ellie's first job. It seemed ideal, a lovely family and a beautiful place to live. Holidays abroad were promised, and the money was higher than the usual rate.

Although Ellie had asked for a contract at the interview it seemed to have been forgotten and she was embarrassed to bring the subject up again.

She was shocked one Monday morning, after she had been there only two months, to be told that the family no longer required her services as the previous nanny would be returning at the end of the week and would she please leave by Thursday lunchtime.

1 Should Ellie have started this job without a contract?
2 How would having a contract have helped her in this situation?
3 Where might Ellie turn for help?

If you have gained employment in another country, a contract is even more important, but will differ in many respects to one that is suitable for working in the UK. The Recruitment and Employment Federation will provide for its member agencies a sample contract for those wishing to work abroad.

You will need to check very carefully that you have all the correct documentation, such as visas and work permits. You might also need a course of immunisations to protect against various illnesses. Going abroad means that you are far away from family, friends and known sources of help, so working abroad is not suitable for a first job.

PANN's advice to nannies seeking employment abroad is:

- never accept an overseas post without first having met the employer
- never travel on a one-way ticket
- never accept an overseas post without a written signed contract
- always maintain contact with the agency back in the UK
- make sure the post you are applying for is for a nanny and not an au pair or mother's help
- use an agency that specialises in overseas placements.

The job description

You will need to be clear about the range of duties and responsibilities that you are expected to carry out. This will be the unique job description that only the family can write. It should state the names and ages of the children to be under your care and list the duties you are expected to undertake. The areas covered might include any of the following:

- activities at home
- outside arrangements, education, leisure
- keeping records
- safety (indoors, garden, outings, car)
- birthday parties
- managing behaviour
- health screening (clinics, routine checks, dentist)
- hygiene
- rest periods
- exercise
- domestic arrangements (clothes, bedding, cleaning, meals)
- managing petty cash
- security of the home
- answering the telephone
- communication with parents
- additional agreed duties.

Once you have agreed the job description, the employer should not make changes without your consent. If they do, and you do not agree with the changes, they must by law offer redundancy, in which case you would be entitled to redundancy pay if you had worked for a qualifying period of time.

Once you have been offered the job, it is time to sit down with your employers to discuss the contract and job description. A young person with little experience may not find this easy to do, but failing to do so may result in unhappiness. Disappointments often occur on both sides because certain tricky issues have not been adequately discussed, and people enter into a contract with different expectations. For example, have you agreed on the amount of housework that is appropriate? Some nannies would not expect to do any chores unrelated to the care of the child, whereas another would take on a wider range of duties. Have you sorted out where you will have your meals, and who is responsible for providing them? Are you limited in your use of the telephone? How welcoming will the family be to your friends? Are they sometimes permitted to sleep over? How do they feel about your boyfriends being in the house?

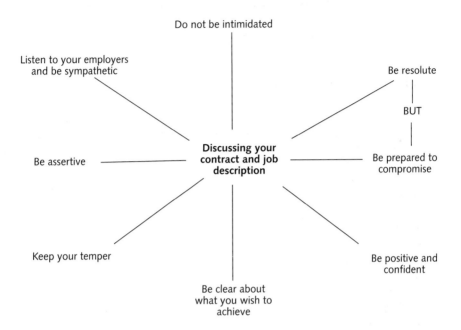

Discussing your contract and job description

CASE STUDY

The parents forgot to mention at interview that Roy, the six-year-old, had a pet rat. When Josephine, the nanny, came face to face with Roy's pet during their first meal together, she had hysterics, frightening the rat who hid under the bed in her room, refusing to budge. When the parents returned home, they found an empty house, and a note on the kitchen table stating that Josephine had taken the children to the local café, where she would wait until the situation was resolved. She refused to enter the house until the rat was removed. In the end, a compromise was reached. Roy's grandmother, who lives in the next road, agreed to look after the rat, and Josephine takes Roy to visit every day after school.

1 How could this situation have been avoided?
2 Was this compromise fair on Roy and on his grandmother?
3 Can you think of an alternative solution to the problem?

The care and time that goes into your job search, preparation for interview and the interview itself, together with thoughtful decision-making and negotiation, should ensure that the job will be a happy and successful experience for you, your employers and the children. However careful you have been, learning to live with another family can be challenging, and you will need to be flexible in your attitudes and willing to compromise on occasions, as long as this does not harm the children.

3 SETTLING IN

This chapter includes:
- **Starting out**
- **Getting to know your family**
- **Exploring the local environment**
- **Support systems**
- **The probationary period**

Everyone is nervous and anxious before starting any new employment. You may have had the advantage of settling in to four or five placements during your training. You know how important first impressions are, and you will arrive punctually, wearing suitable clothes, willing and eager to learn and to fit in with the family.

Starting out

Wherever you work, you are aware of the importance of professional behaviour and attitudes. You know that you will be reliable and punctual, contacting your employer if unavoidably delayed or sick. When both parents work, it is vitally important that you arrive in good time, as otherwise they will be late for their own job. Most employers agree that their best nannies have been cheerful, enthusiastic, child-centred and active, but the two really important qualities are reliability and punctuality. Good nannies have to have a strong work ethic, being conscientious and hard-working.

CASE STUDY

Kathryn lives four miles from the family she works for and the journey on public transport can take the best part of an hour. One day she woke up with a headache and a sore throat. She rang her employer to say she was not feeling well, to be told that both parents had important meetings that day, and could she possibly come in just to supervise the children. They agreed to pay for a taxi both ways. Kathryn spent the day lying on the sofa watching the children play with their toys.

1 Should Kathryn have gone in to work:
  a) from the children's point of view
  b) for her own health needs?
2 What might have happened had she refused?
3 Do you think the employers were fair?
4 Was there an alternative solution?

All nannies are responsible for:

- ensuring the safety and wellbeing of the children
- being sensitive to the individual needs of the children
- preparing, establishing and maintaining a learning environment that encourages the all-round development of the children
- observing, assessing and monitoring the progress of the children
- regularly communicating with parents, respecting their greater knowledge of the child
- keeping up to date with current issues in childcare and education
- ensuring equality of opportunity for all children, respecting and valuing each child as an individual.

Nannies have always been seen as protectors and carers of children by their employers. Your knowledge of developmental needs and the importance of providing stimulating activities may not be fully appreciated. Once you are in employment, it is up to you to be more vocal about this important aspect of your work.

You will have met the family at interview, and perhaps since, and seen the accommodation prepared for you if you are residential. You will have ensured that you have a contract of employment, and have clear guidelines as to the child-rearing practices of your particular family. If this is the first time you have left home, you might be missing your own family and friends, and familiar surroundings. Your employer will be aware of this, and make allowances for it. Your professionalism will not allow you to be miserable while you are working with the children, and if anyone can lift your spirits, children can.

If you are travelling to work every day, you need to ensure that you have allowed plenty of time for traffic and possible delays, for there is nothing as unsettling as arriving late on your first day in a new job.

Getting to know your family

On the day agreed for you to start your new post, it is probably a good idea to suggest that you and your employer might have a couple of hours together. You might like to ask to see some photographs of the children when they were babies and start asking about their characteristics and personalities. Starting your relationship in a relaxed fashion does not mean that you will be 'best friends': it is starting a relationship with trust and respect that will allow you to work together efficiently and to communicate regularly about the children. Having previously photocopied the 'Care needs' chart on pages 30–31, completing the chart together with the family will help you to remember each child's individual needs. You will need to do one for each child.

Your employer will no doubt give you a tour of the house, pointing out any rooms she would prefer you and the children not to use in her absence, such as her bedroom, study and any area that is dangerous. Be aware of any smoke alarms, fire extinguishers and other safety equipment such as the first aid box, fire blankets, and where to exit if there should be a fire.

During the tour find out where the telephones are located. Ask how the family would like the phone to be answered and how and when the answer phone is to be used. Ask to be shown where the fuse box and gas, water and electricity meters are to be found.

You will need to know how all the kitchen equipment works: the cooker, the dishwasher, the washer, the dryer and any other smaller electrical gadgets such as the toaster or the kettle.

While in the kitchen, you can discuss mealtimes and when you are expected to eat with the family and when they would prefer you to eat with the children. Mention any dietary needs you may have.

Your family will expect you to keep both the home and the children safe while they are at work. Familiarise yourself with the alarm system, if there is one, and practice setting it and turning it off. Make sure the home is secure, check that all windows and doors are closed and locked when going out, and look after your keys carefully. Find out if a neighbour has a spare set of keys in case of difficulty.

Much of the information you are receiving may not be immediately understood, and some may be quickly forgotten, as it is very difficult to take in a great deal of new knowledge when you are new to a situation. For this reason we have compiled the chart on page 32 which you can photocopy and fill in with your employer at a later date.

The sooner you get to know your family and their regular routines, the quicker you will feel at ease. You might find it useful, as the job is new, to sit down with your employer and complete a chart similar to the 'The family routine' chart on page 33. This will help you to understand the structure of the family's week, and your contribution to it.

The parents will find it reassuring if you keep a daily diary, perhaps as outlined in the 'Daily information for parents' chart on page 33. They may wish to add other areas to this information sheet. This will help you and the parents to act in partnership, meeting the needs of the children, and ensuring continuity of care.

Care needs	
Child's name:	**Notes**
Toileting How often is the nappy changed? Where is it changed? What is used to clean the baby? How do you know when s/he needs to use the lavatory? Are there any unusual signals or words used? Is a nappy used at night?	
Food Does s/he have any allergies? Where does s/he eat? Is s/he given food choices? Is s/he expected to finish the meal? What happens if s/he refuses food? What table manners are expected?	
Dressing Who dresses him/her? Who chooses the clothes to be worn? Does s/he like privacy? Can s/he tie her own shoelaces?	
Separation How does s/he cope with separation? How is s/he distracted? How does s/he like to be comforted when distressed?	
Behaviour What is to be done when s/he is misbehaving? What is to be done when s/he is not co-operating?	

Care needs *continued*	Notes
Rituals Is there a special way of doing things at bath time, bedtime, rest time and mealtimes? Does s/he have a comfort object?	
Preferences Book Toy Food Drink Person Game Activity	
Friends Who is allowed to visit? Where do they play? Can s/he play at a friend's house, with or without prior permission?	
Domestic What chores is s/he expected to do?	
Activities Time on the computer Homework Watching TV Music practice Outside activities	
Medical concerns Past illnesses	

Home information

SECURITY

Tick box for yes.

Do you know how to secure the home (doors, windows shutters)? ❑

Do you know how to set the alarm? ❑

Do you know where to find a spare set of keys? ❑

SAFETY

Where to find the:

Fire extinguisher ....

Torch ....

Candles ....

Fuse box ....

First Aid kit ....

EMERGENCY telephone numbers:

Doctor .... Vet ....

Gas .... Water ....

Electricity .... Local authority ....

....

RUBBISH DISPOSAL

Arrangements for disposal of rubbish:

....

....

DOMESTIC EQUIPMENT

How to use the:

Washing machine ....

Drier ....

Microwave ....

Cooker ....

Dishwasher ....

Central heating ....

Other essential information ....

....

The family routine			
	Morning	**Afternoon**	**Evening**
Mon	11–11.30 Hannah swimming	Martin works from home	7–8 Clare to Amnesty meeting
Tues	9.30–12 Hannah playgroup	4.30 William football practice	
Wed	9.30–12 Hannah playgroup	2–3.30 Josh toddler group	Martin home late
Thurs	9.30–12 Hannah playgroup		6–7 Martin to gym
Fri		Clare finishes work 3.00 Takes William swimming	Parents out. Babysitting
Sat	Granny often visits		
Sun	Church		

Daily information for parents	
Date	Tuesday 2 May
Sleep	Josh slept for an hour this morning.
Toileting	No accidents today!
Health	Josh seems a little off-colour today. No temp. though.
Meals	Both had cheese sandwiches and fruit for lunch and fish fingers, green beans and new potatoes for tea. Hannah still not keen on beans but she ate a small portion.
Play	Hannah and I did some painting while Josh slept this morning. We all went to the park this afternoon. Josh really likes his new socks.
Social	We met Jake and Fiona at the park. The children get on well together.
New skills	Hannah can tie her shoelaces now — with help! Her painting is lovely — her faces now have noses (see corkboard). William scored 2 goals in match.
Behaviour	Both OK today. Minor squabbles over toys this morning.
Comments	The fence at the back of the garden is very splintery. Perhaps now that the weather is picking up we could get some more outdoor toys for the garden?

Another useful chart for you to complete is a medical and emergency information chart (see page 35). You will feel happier if you have at your fingertips the names, addresses and telephone numbers of whom to contact if the parents are not available.

During the first week of the job, you will find yourself constantly asking your employer questions, such as, 'How does the washing machine work?' 'Where does this belong?' 'Where do I find the iron?' But you will soon become familiar and comfortable with the home and the family.

A recent survey shows some of the issues that might seem trifling to you but may be important to your family. These include:
■ coming home to a tidy house, with no dirty cups in the kitchen sink
■ finding the bathroom clean
■ personal hygiene
■ expecting you to be fully dressed before you start work
■ a courteous approach when answering the telephone.

Find out how your employers would like to be addressed, either by first names, or more formally, and agree how the parents and the children will address you.

One of your prime responsibilities will be to ensure a safe and hazard-free environment for the children in your charge. If there are hazards, discuss them

Medical/emergency information
Full names of children and dates of birth
Mother's name: Place of work: Telephone number: Mobile number:
Father's name: Place of work: Telephone number: Mobile number:
Family doctor: Address: Telephone number:
Contact if parents not available: Name: Address: Telephone number: Relationship:
Hospital of choice in an emergency: Address: Telephone number:
Health visitor: Address: Telephone number:
Children's allergies:
Children's medication:
Immunisation status:
Other essential information:

tactfully with your employer at an appropriate time, pointing out the possible risks to the children. It may not be possible to make everything safe right away, either because of cost, or the personal views of the parents. Always be positive when pointing out a problem, and offer a possible solution. You have done your professional duty by pointing out health and safety risks, and you are aware of what risks there are, and will attempt to minimise them, and keep the children safe.

Activity
You are to work with a family of three children, aged four months, two and a half years, and seven years. You will be given the use of a car. Research the various restraints that are available and suitable for the ages of the children. What other safety and insurance aspects may you need to consider?

The first few days are an important time for you and the family. There is a lot to learn about the house, the family and the locality. There is also a lot for you to learn about the way in which your family operates, their likes and dislikes and their lifestyle.

Exploring the local environment

If you are new to the area, ask your employer to point out:
- the local shops
- the doctor's surgery
- the local health clinic
- the hospital
- the pre-school and/or school
- the library
- the park
- bus stops
- the underground station or train station
- petrol stations (if you have the use of a car)
- local leisure amenities
- the homes of any member of the family or best friends.

If your new job is in an environment totally alien to you, you might find this very stressful. If you have always lived in the country, but longed to live in the city, you might find the noise, traffic, busy lifestyle and general pollution harder to live with than you would have imagined. It can take time to adapt.

Moving from an urban area into a quiet country village can also demand a period of adjustment. You may have longed for the peace and quiet of the countryside, but find the reality very different. Little public transport, few places of entertainment, few activities for under-fives might have you yearning for the busy life you have left behind.

Susan had never been away from home before and found the busy city a frightening place. She took a job as a live-in nanny caring for a small baby and a four-year old. Travelling on the underground to take the older child to a pre-school group was stressful. She could not sleep at night because of the noise of the traffic. She spent the evenings in her room feeling very depressed and tearful.

After a week her father telephoned to see how she was getting on. She burst into tears and said she wanted to come home. Her father, having ascertained that she liked the family, suggested she stuck it out for at least four weeks before handing in her notice, as it would not look good on her CV if she gave up so easily.

At the end of the month, everything looked different. She had made friends and was becoming used to the hustle and bustle of city life.

She stayed with the family for another five years.

1 How could Susan have been more prepared for such a change of lifestyle?
2 Should the family have been aware of what was happening?
3 How might the family have helped Susan?

You will probably need guidance for the first few months if you are new to the neighbourhood so as to learn what facilities are available. It may be a good idea to find out whether there are any guidebooks available locally; some towns have booklets listing facilities and activities for under-fives.

If you are allowed the use of a car, the parents may wish to drive with you, so that they can assess your driving skills, and make sure that you drive safely and competently. If you have only just passed your test, and it is an essential part of the job that you drive the children on occasion, you might feel happier if you take some further driving lessons. The insurance implications are outlined in Chapter 14.

Support systems

Once settled, you will want to build a social life for yourself and the children. There are many ways of doing this. If the children are attending pre-school or school, you will meet other carers, who may be parents or nannies. If the children are friends, you may well become friends too. If the children are younger, seek out mother and toddler groups, or other facilities for the youngest children, where you will have to accompany them, thus meeting other people. Many locations where there are several nannies employed have nanny circles, where they welcome new faces. There are also some self-help groups for nannies working in more isolated settings.

You may have the unfortunate experience of being the nanny in a family where one of the children dies or develops a terminal illness. The family often receives comfort and counselling from friends and professionals, but the trauma the nanny has suffered is often overlooked. She is left feeling isolated, and unable to express her feelings of grief. A service to help such nannies was started by Paula Jackson in 1998. It is called Lean on Me, and can be reached on 01483 577 232. Paula will put you in touch with another carer who has experienced a similar situation and will listen to you for as long as you want, and hopefully be of some comfort. A booklet she has written will be published in 2001, and is endorsed by PANN.

Nannies working alone often feel isolated and lonely. In some urban areas where there are large numbers of nannies employed, you will find nanny 'networks' developing. This will be a social group of like-minded people who perhaps take it in turns to entertain in the family home, or who organise outings, either with the children, or without them in the evenings. Many close friendships are formed in this way. If you are new to an area, contacting a local nanny agency may be a way of linking in to a local group. Be careful, when talking about your family, that you do not disclose any confidential information.

If you are working in the country, and there seem to be few nannies in employment in your village and few appropriate organisations to join, you might try putting an advertisement in *Nursery World*, inviting other nannies in similar circumstances to get in touch. Support groups themselves often advertise in the local press and in *Nursery World*.

You might consider joining evening classes to learn a new skill, a craft or a language. You could improve or update your academic qualifications. If there is no local adult education college, or it is difficult for you to be released for a particular course, you might think of enroling for an Open University course. You would be working in isolation for most of the year, but most OU courses require you to attend a summer school, with the opportunity to meet the other students on your course.

UNIONS AND PROFESSIONAL ASSOCIATIONS

Every employee has the legal right to join an independent trade union. Any employer who interferes with this right can be ordered to pay compensation to the employee. Employees can belong to any trade union they like, except where membership is limited to particular occupations or skills. Car mechanics would be rejected if wanting to join PANN. It is sensible to join a union or a professional association for a number of reasons. It provides a safety net in times of difficulty, arguing your case against dismissal, giving legal protection, support and advice, and will represent you in negotiating pay and conditions of service. Many unions and professional associations offer inexpensive or even free insurance cover. A union represents its members in improving working conditions and protecting the interests of their members, for example in health and safety issues, pensions and security. It might take on a campaigning role. It will ensure that employers live up to their responsibilities to their employees.

The main union that nannies join is PANN (Professional Association of Nursery Nurses), 2 St. James' Court, Friar Gate, Derby, DE1 lDT (telephone: 01332 372337). PANN was formed in 1982 and is a section of PAT (Professional

Association of Teachers), representing the interests of professional and student childcare practitioners employed within education, social services, the health service and the private sector, including nannies. The current membership is 6,000 and is open to qualified childcare practitioners holding the DCE/CACHE qualifications, BTEC Diploma, NVQ3 or the NAMCW. Membership is also open to childcare practitioners who have obtained at least three years relevant experience without obtaining a recognised qualification, and who can supply two professional references.

PANN differs from other trade unions in that it positively opposes strike action, it never involves children in disputes, and it gives priority to 'professionalism'. It is not affiliated to the TUC, and does not pay a levy to any political party.

In June, 1995, it decided to join forces with the Professional Association of Teachers and form a nursery nurse section of PAT. The benefits include legal advice and protection, and personal liability insurance cover against actions brought alleging injury to persons or damage to property during the course of employment, or while engaged in recognised extracurricula activities. There are opportunities to obtain home and car insurance, a PAT Visa card with no annual fee, and group RAC membership.

The probationary period

Most contracts will include a probationary period, when both you and your employer can assess how well you are succeeding in your job, how happy you are with the family, and whether you both want to continue to work together. Approximately two weeks before the end of the set probationary period, it will be useful to you if you complete the check list on page 40.

As the induction period progresses you will begin to get to know each other quite well. You need to establish a professional relationship: you will not expect to be treated as a guest in the house, but as an important employee. You should not be expected to take on any task that your employer would not do herself. You will be developing an honest, trusting relationship.

Assessing the probationary period

I have shown:

punctuality	Yes ❑	No ❑
maturity	Yes ❑	No ❑
good judgement	Yes ❑	No ❑
professionalism	Yes ❑	No ❑
initiative	Yes ❑	No ❑
enthusiasm	Yes ❑	No ❑
care and kindliness	Yes ❑	No ❑
good health.	Yes ❑	No ❑
I am seen as part of the family.	Yes	
I enjoy being with the children.	Yes	
I am familiar with and apply rules of safety.	Yes ❑	No ❑
I am familiar with emergency procedures.	Yes ❑	No ❑
We have settled negotiable issues in a professional way.	Yes ❑	No ❑
The children respond well to me.	Yes ❑	No ❑
I provide a range of activities for the children.	Yes ❑	No ❑
I have established good routines.	Yes ❑	No ❑
I get on well with the family.	Yes ❑	No ❑
I communicate well with the family and their friends.	Yes ❑	No ❑

4 *ROUTINES*

Routines refer to regular events, organised and planned within the day, such as hygiene practices, mealtimes, nap times, exercise and play. It is impossible to generalise and describe a family's day, as each one will be unique. Much depends on the ages and the number of the children, the established family routines, and personal preferences. Obviously, if you are caring for a school-age child, one of your routines will be taking and collecting her from school.

Routines should take place at the same time each day, so that the young child feels secure by knowing what to expect. Routines set boundaries so that both you and the children understand the limits to their behaviour. A nanny who is constantly changing her daily routines, and allowing herself to be overwhelmed by events, will find the children becoming fractious or distressed. For this reason, you will need to arrange your routines carefully, allowing enough time for each one. Although not so tightly scheduled, you will also need to reflect on weekly routines, such as on what day the older child has a music lesson, on monthly routines, which might include a major shopping trip, or getting the children's hair cut, and yearly routines, such as preparing for summer holidays. Time management is an issue for all nannies. The day can be very busy and complex, and there needs to be time built in for unforeseen events and for giving 'quality time' to individual children.

Undoubtedly, you will have to fit in some domestic routines in your busy day. Encourage the children to help you as this will lead to independence and teach them how to clear up after themselves. Many routine tasks can contribute to children's development and learning. For example, walking to school presents an opportunity for exercise and conversation and may expand the child's knowledge of the outside world.

> **Activity**
> Think about all your personal routines. Devise a weekly and monthly chart, showing the essential routines. How do these match the needs of a family where the children are aged six months, three years and seven years?

Routine physical care

Some routines require physical care. These include skin and hair care, sleep and rest, exercise, care of the teeth, and hygiene practices, such as hand washing and toileting. Most young children need adult help and supervision in their personal care requirements. Good standards of care are important to prevent ill health, to increase self-esteem and gain acceptance by other children. The eventual goal is for the children to become independent and care for all their physical needs themselves.

SKIN AND HAIR CARE

Nannies should:
- ensure that the children wash their hands and faces before and after handling and eating food
- ensure they wash their hands after using the lavatory and after messy play
- observe the skin for any rashes or sores
- play a part in moisturising the skin of children, taking advice from parents
- protect the skin from excessive exposure to the sun, using hats, sun block or high-factor sun cream

- play a part in treating skin problems, such as eczema and sweat rash, following discussion with the parents.

Hair will vary in colour, texture and style. There can be strong religious and cultural practices associated with care of the hair and you may need to discuss these with the parents.

When you wash children's hair, use a non-stinging gentle shampoo, rinse the hair well, and avoid using the hair dryer. Prevention is better than cure, so have at hand some shower caps for the children when playing with sand, or with any other very messy material. Regular brushing and combing will discourage head lice. Once children are in constant contact with other children, their hair needs to be checked regularly for signs of head lice (nits).

SLEEP AND REST

It is most important to establish a routine for bedtime. From the youngest age, children need to know when bedtime is inevitable. You can help this by:
- bathing them at the same time each night
- having a light snack and a drink of milk before cleaning their teeth
- making sure they have been to the lavatory
- creating a restful atmosphere in the bedroom by drawing the curtains, turning down the beds and clearing toys away
- reading a familiar story that is not frightening or stimulating
- singing some familiar songs
- making sure they have their comfort objects
- listening to a taped story. This is more suitable for older children.

Like adults, children appear to need differing amounts of sleep. You will need to discuss the sleep routines of babies and children with the parents. Children will sleep better if they have had plenty of fresh air and exercise during the day. Sometimes older children may be resistant to this, if they are constantly watching television or playing games on the computer.

Sleep allows the body to rest and recover from its exertions, so it is important that children are encouraged to rest after vigorous physical exercise. Sleep consists of deep relaxing sleep and rapid eye movement (REM) sleep, when we dream. It is thought that children use REM sleep to make sense of their day, and if they are woken at this time they may become drowsy and disorientated.

Some children are wakeful during the night and are used to going into their parent's bed for a cuddle. If one of the children wants to get into your bed, this should not be allowed. Apart from disturbing your sleep, you may be laying yourself open to accusations of abuse.

Children need to unwind and relax before they are able to sleep. Even if children do not sleep during the day, there should still be a quiet period when they can look at books or just have a cuddle.

EXERCISE AND FRESH AIR

Making sure that children exercise every day will help them to establish this as a habit for life and may prevent future heart disease and obesity. Access to a garden is obviously a great help in promoting fresh air and exercise, but even without one, it is possible to take the children to a park or playground regularly. School children should be encouraged to take part in sporting activities outside school hours, if this is at all possible.

CARE OF THE TEETH

Nannies, in consultation with parents, play a part in encouraging good dental hygiene. They will:

- encourage children to brush their teeth after meals, using their own brush that is changed at least every three months and a fluoride toothpaste
- provide a healthy diet, low in sugar, high in vitamins and calcium
- avoid giving sweet drinks, especially in a bottle or on a dummy
- restrict giving sweets to children
- not give sweet snacks between meals
- be aware that food such as apples, carrots and brown bread, that has to be chewed, is good for healthy teeth.

You may be expected to take the children for regular dental checks. In partnership with the parents, prepare them carefully, discussing what is likely to happen, perhaps finding a book at the library about visiting the dentist. If you are nervous at the dentist, be careful not to pass any of your fears and anxieties on to the children.

TOILET TRAINING

There are many different theories and methods of toilet training, and you will need to discuss this fully with the parents. Successful toilet training requires a consistent approach between you and the parents. Toilet training can start when the child is ready, generally between eighteen months and two years. Children are usually not ready before this because their central nervous system is not sufficiently developed to alert them to the fact that their bowel or bladder is full, and they also do not have the language to express their urgent needs. If the child is pressurised too early, toilet training can develop into a battle. To be successful you should:

- be relaxed and not show disapproval about any 'accidents'
- let the child see other children or adults using the lavatory
- leave a potty available before you intend the child to use it, so that it becomes familiar
- if you see signs of a bowel movement, offer the potty but without any pressure for the child to use it
- congratulate the child and show pleasure when the potty is used
- be aware that training is easier in the summer when the child is wearing fewer clothes.

Once a child is trained, she may still need reminding to use the lavatory, particularly before going to sleep or going out. Accidents can still happen, and you should not make a fuss, but keep some spare pants available if you are going out.

1 Nannies should be a positive role model.
2 Establish routines that promote hygiene.
3 Make keeping clean fun, by putting toys in the bath, having 'fun' toothbrushes and flavoured toothpaste.
4 Make sure each child has her own flannel, toothbrush, towel and comb.
5 Provide a footstool, so that the younger children can reach the basin comfortably and sit on the lavatory without fear of falling through the hole.
6 Teach children to care for themselves, and encourage independence in routines.

Mealtimes and nutrition

It is important for you to have a good understanding of nutrition and how to provide a well-balanced diet for the children in your care. A healthy nutritious diet plays a large part in promoting health, and in ensuring healthy development. The way you cook and eat, and the food you provide, will help the children to develop sensible eating patterns and will encourage children to try various types of food.

To be and remain healthy you need to have a wholesome balanced diet. To provide a balanced diet, you need to know what the body requires, and this will depend on age, gender, and how much exercise you take. You will need some understanding of what is contained in different types of food. The body needs energy to keep alive, to breathe, to grow and to keep warm. This energy comes from food. The more active the person, the more energy will be used.

Eating patterns are established at a very early age. Part of your role in caring for children will include providing food and drinks, educating them in eating healthily, understanding the main rules of nutrition, and being a good role model by setting a good example when you are eating with the children.

A HEALTHY DIET

Food consists of substances known as nutrients. Without food we could not exist. The main nutrients in food and drink are:
- carbohydrates
- proteins
- fats
- vitamins
- minerals
- fibre
- water.

Proteins, carbohydrates, fats and water are present in large amounts in our food and are known as macro-nutrients. Vitamins and minerals are only present in small amounts and are known as micro-nutrients.

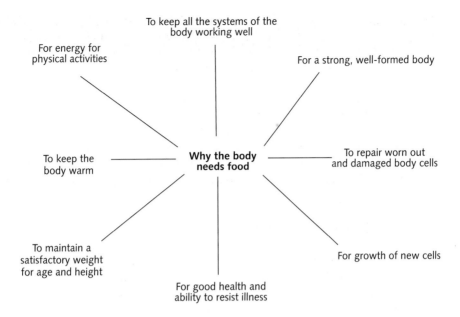

To keep all the systems of the body working well

For energy for physical activities

For a strong, well-formed body

To keep the body warm

Why the body needs food

To repair worn out and damaged body cells

To maintain a satisfactory weight for age and height

For growth of new cells

For good health and ability to resist illness

Why the body needs food

A balanced diet consists of a variety of foods from all the above nutrients. Care must be taken not to overeat, particularly saturated fats and sugars, but to eat sufficient to meet your needs. The more energetic you are, the more calories (units of energy) you will burn up, and the more food you will need. Energy is required by all living things to maintain the changes and chemical reactions that occur in the body (metabolism).

Foods that have little water and a high proportion of fat or carbohydrate have a high energy value. Children need more kilocalories because their bodies are growing and they use a lot of energy. The kilocalories required will vary according to age, gender, size, physical activity and climate.

A variety of fresh foods daily in adequate amounts, from the following food groups, should be offered to children every day:

■ bread, cereal, rice and pasta
■ vegetables and fruits
■ fats and sugars
■ milk, yoghurt and cheese
■ meat, poultry, fish, eggs, beans and pulses.

To allow for their healthy growth and development children have different food needs to adults. No single food can supply all the nutrients required by a child.

Milk is an important food for children as it contains all the major nutrients needed, except for iron and vitamin C. Drinking too much milk may reduce the appetite for other important foods.

Children need a certain amount of fat in their diet to provide energy and the necessary vitamins. It is as well to offer less fat from animal sources, and more vegetable fat, such as frying food with oil instead of butter. Too much animal fat in the diet may lead to heart problems in later life. Water is an important nutrient and should be offered several times a day, instead of sugared drinks.

Fibre is necessary in preventing constipation. Fibre is found in brown rice, wholemeal bread or pasta, baked beans, pulses, potato skins, fruit and vegetables. Small children find it difficult to digest a great deal of fibre and should never be given a high-fibre diet, but it can be offered in small amounts as a snack.

Fruits and vegetables are good sources of vitamins, minerals and fibre especially when eaten raw. A variety is necessary, as they all contain different vitamins. It is recommended that everyone eats at least five portions of fruits and vegetables every day, whether they are fresh, frozen or tinned.

Breads and cereals, especially whole grain products, are an important source of vitamin B and iron, and supply some protein. Nuts provide protein but can be a safety hazard for young children, because of the risk of choking. Parents need to be asked if a child has an allergy to nuts including peanut butter. Some children may be allergic to other foods, such as strawberries and shellfish.

There are concerns about the use of food additives. These are usually chemicals that are added to food to stop it from going bad, and help it to look and taste good. It is thought that some additives contribute to hyperactivity and allergies. Parents should advise you if they wish you to exclude certain foods from their child's diet. Many processed foods and drinks contain many additives, including salt and sugar. Looking at the labels will inform you of the amount and type of additives used in the product.

There is a view that some children, particularly younger children, or children who are unwell, benefit if they eat little and often. Snacks should certainly be offered if children are hungry, but try and discourage children from snacking less than two hours before a meal as it might spoil their appetite for the main meal. Some examples of wholesome and enjoyable snacks are:

- water, milk and fresh fruit juices (diluted with water to prevent tooth enamel rotting)
- fresh fruit
- dried fruit such as apricots (good source of iron), prunes and figs
- vegetable sticks, such as carrots, celery and cucumber
- houmous
- yoghurt
- crackers
- oatmeal biscuits
- rice cakes.

Use sugar in moderation, as sugar can lead to tooth decay and obesity. If you are cooking with the children, try to cook something other than cakes and biscuits. Salt should be used sparingly in cooking, and should not be put on the table for children to help themselves.

It is quite common these days for families to be vegetarian, and exclude meat and perhaps fish from the diet.

If your usual diet is different from that of the family you will need to decide if you will be happy complying with the diet of the family. This issue should be

raised at interview. Conversely, if you are a vegetarian, you must feel able to respect the wishes of the family if you are asked to cook and prepare meat and fish for the children.

The first three years of life are a period of rapid growth and protein is needed to support this growth, and allow the bones and the brain to develop properly. Children also require a high intake of calories to provide energy for physical activity. If the calories needed for energy are not provided by carbohydrates and fat, then protein will be used to provide energy rather than being used for growth.

The Department of Health recommends one pint of whole milk daily for children under five years, particularly for its fat and vitamin content. This can be offered in a variety of ways: in puddings, custard, yoghurt and cheese, as well as on cereal or as a drink. Sugar should never be added to children's food and drinks, and foods containing a great deal of sugar such as biscuits, pastries and jams should be offered only occasionally in small quantities.

SPECIAL DIETS

Some children that you may care for may be on a special diet. Special diets are worked out by the doctor and dietician according to the individual needs of the child. It is important that you find out as much as you can about the condition and encourage and support the child on a special diet. Under no circumstances must you give the child anything that she is not allowed.

Some children, not suffering from any particular disorder (see page 50), may be restricted in their diet in certain foods. For example, children who may have

Common disorders that require a special diet

Condition	Description	Diet
Coeliac disease	Sensitivity to gluten, a protein found in wheat, rye, barley and oats. Child fails to thrive	Exclude all foods containing gluten. Can eat fresh fruit and vegetables, fish, meat and dairy produce
Cystic fibrosis	An inherited condition, sticky thick mucus is found in the lungs and digestive system. Interferes with the digestion of food	Tablets given to help the digestion. Needs a high-protein, high-calorie diet
Diabetes	The body fails to produce enough insulin to control the amount of sugar in the body	Regular meals, diet carefully balanced and controlled. May need a snack before exercise, should be observed closely
Obesity	Overweight for height and age	Plan, offer and encourage a healthy balanced diet. Discourage over-eating. Encourage daily exercise
Anaemia	Lack of iron in the diet. Can also be caused by severe blood loss	A diet high in red meat, liver, eggs, cocoa, green vegetables, apricots, helped by taking Vitamin C at the same time
Cows' milk allergy: • to protein • lactose (milk sugar) intolerance	Associated with family history of allergy. Can result in wheezing, diarrhoea, vomiting, rashes, abdominal pain and tiredness	Special formula milk for babies. Substitute milks for older children. Avoid cows' milk, cheese and yoghurt

frequent chesty illnesses, might be rationed in their intake of milk, and offered fruit juice instead. Some children may have serious allergic reactions to some foods, leading to an anaphylactic shock. This is a generalised allergic reaction that may occur a few minutes after eating a particular food, such as peanuts. It can also occur after injecting a drug or being stung by an insect. It is rare, but knowledge of First Aid is essential as the air passages become constricted and the swelling of the face and neck increase the risk of suffocation.

Food intolerances are more common than severe allergies. For example, intolerance to dairy food may lead to stomach upsets and an intolerance to peppers can cause migraine. Parents will usually be aware of what foods are to be avoided, and you will need to be equally on your guard, especially if you are taking the children out to eat. Parents of children who are very active may wish to reduce the amount of additives their children eat and drink, as it is thought that some additives contribute to hyperactivity.

CASE STUDY

Patricia is a young qualified nanny, having recently gained her Diploma in Childcare and Education. She has spent four years in College and is enjoying her first job, looking after a baby, a toddler and a six-year-old.

Her employer has gone back to work, leaving Patricia caring for the children from eight o'clock in the morning to six o'clock in the evening. There is one problem: Patricia has never learnt how to cook. She understands how important it is to give the children a wholesome balanced diet, and for the first week feeds them on salads, fresh fruit, sandwiches and cold meat.

The six-year-old gets fed up with this diet and complains to his parents.

1 Why do you think Patricia never learnt to cook?
2 What can Patricia do about learning to cook?
3 How might the parent help Patricia?

Many diets are linked to religious practices. The table on page 52 indicates the main religions, and the foods they do not eat.

Some religions have special days when food is forbidden. This must always be respected and allowance made for the children feeling tired. They may need to rest more often than usual.

Food hygiene

Many foods carry germs that grow in warm, moist conditions. Eggs and chickens can be infected with salmonella, a bacterium that can cause food poisoning. Cheeses grow moulds. Milk goes bad, particularly if not kept in the fridge. Raw meat contains many different bacteria and needs to be carefully handled. Food poisoning can be caused by:

■ salmonella (germs that usually live in the bowels of humans or animals, or may be found in water polluted by sewage). If food that contains salmonella is cooked thoroughly the germs will be killed and not cause any harm. Care also

Dietary customs

Food	Jewish	Sikh	Muslim	Hindu	Buddhist	7th Day Adventist	Rastafarian	Roman Catholic	Mormon
Eggs	No blood spots	✓	✓	Some	Some	Most	✓	✓	✓
Milk/yoghurt	Not with meat	✓	Not with rennet	Not with rennet	✓	Most	✓	✓	✓
Cheese	Not with meat	Some	Some	Some	✓	Most	✓	✓	✓
Chicken	Kosher	Some	Halal	Some	✗	Some	Some	Some still prefer not to eat meat on Fridays, particularly during Lent	✓
Mutton/lamb	Kosher	✓	Halal	Some	✗	Some	Some		✓
Beef	Kosher	✗	Halal	✗	✗	Some	Some		✓
Pork	✗	Rarely	✗	Rarely	✗	✗	✗	✓	✓
Fish	With scales, fins and back-bone	Some	Halal	With fins and scales	Some	Some	✓	✓	✓
Shellfish	✗	Some	Halal	Some	✗	✗	✗	✓	✓
Animal fats	Kosher	Some	Some Halal	Some	✗	✗	Some	✓	✓
Alcohol	✓	✓	✗	✗	✗	✗	✗	✓	✗
Cocoa/tea/coffee	✓	✓	✓	✓	✓ No milk	✗	✗	✓	✗
Nuts	✓	✓	✓	✓	✓	✓	✓	✓	✓
Pulses	✓	✓	✓	✓	✓	✓	✓	✓	✓
Fruit	✓	✓	✓	✓	✓	✓	✓	✓	✓
Vegetables	✓	✓	✓	✓	✓	✓	✓	✓	✓
Fasting (where not specified, fasting is a matter of individual choice)	Yom Kippur		Ramadan						24 hours once monthly

✓ Accepted   ✗ Forbidden

Adapted from *Nutritional Guidelines*, ILEA, 1985

needs to be taken with personal hygiene. After cleaning a chicken, hands must be carefully washed in an antibacterial soap and all surfaces disinfected

- staphylococcus (germs that may be found in the nose or throat, in boils or septic wounds). If introduced into food, the germs produce poisons that are quite difficult to destroy
- *E. coli*, found in the bowel, that is often passed on because of poor personal hygiene
- listeria, found in dairy products that have not been heated to the temperature required to kill the germs (the process of pasteurisation)

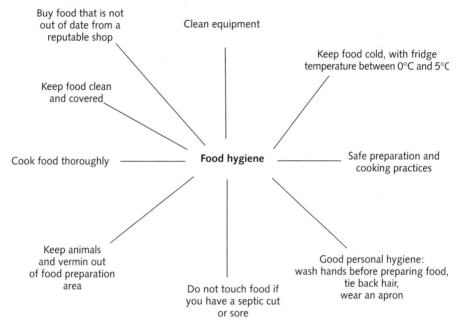

Food hygiene

Some families may have decided against eating meat in response to various food scares. You would of course abide by this rule when preparing food at home and when taking the children out to eat, either in a restaurant or with friends.

When caring for children, it is very important that you have very high standards of personal hygiene and an awareness of how to store and prepare food correctly in order to prevent infection. You must be sure that you and the children wash hands after using the lavatory, handling animals and their equipment, coughing or sneezing, and before preparing and eating food. In addition, you need to wash thoroughly after changing nappies, wiping noses, wiping bottoms and handling raw food. Never touch food if you have been suffering from vomiting or diarrhoea and:

- wash your hands before and after handling food
- keep the kitchen working surfaces, utensils and implements clean
- never re-freeze food that has already been defrosted
- never store raw meat alongside other food. Keep it well wrapped at the bottom of the refrigerator

- have the freezer always set at minus 18 degrees centigrade to prevent germs multiplying
- sterilise feeding bottles and teats for as long as they are used, as germs multiply very quickly in milk
- keep rubbish bins covered and clean
- cover any cuts or sores on your hands with a waterproof dressing or wear gloves.

The use of soap and water, fresh air and sunlight will destroy many germs. Using chemical disinfectants, such as strong bleach, to clean surfaces will destroy germs but will be harmful to children and pets, and needs to be stored locked away. Antiseptics are weak disinfectants that prevent the growth of germs but do not destroy them.

Food should always be bought from shops with a good reputation for freshness. The sell-by date should be clearly shown. Hands should never touch raw food that is not going to be cooked, such as salads, cheese or cooked meats. Use a knife or spoon and fork to serve it.

Symptoms of food poisoning can include diarrhoea, vomiting and stomach ache. Babies must see a doctor immediately, and older children after 24 hours if they have not recovered. Children must be encouraged to drink water to replace water loss.

CHILDREN'S EATING PATTERNS

Eating is a basic human need and an activity that most people enjoy. Apart from being essential for survival it makes you feel good. Eating around the table is a social activity, a time when relaxed conversations can take place, and news of the day shared.

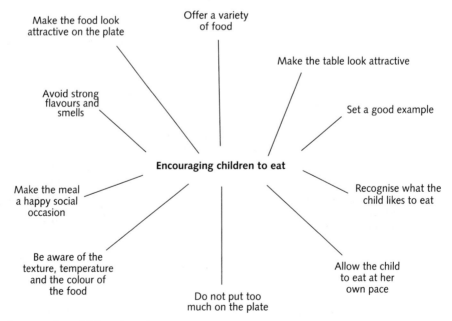

Encouraging children to eat

Children's eating patterns develop from infancy. The attitude to food of the parents and nanny is most important. Adults might show concern and anxiety if a child refuses food, because they worry that the child might not grow and develop well without what they feel is sufficient food. They might feel rejected that the meal they have prepared with such loving care has been refused. The child may discover that whether they eat or not is of very great importance and therefore have a way of manipulating adults.

'Table manners' are more important in some families than in others. Appetites differ in children and are unpredictable. Children know their own hunger signs and it is more sensible to offer smaller portions, and provide more if the child requests it. If children say they are hungry in the middle of the morning, it is wiser to offer them a snack of fruit or raw vegetables, as filling up on milk, bread or biscuits will reduce the appetite for the midday meal.

Children have a shorter attention span than adults. Some find it very hard to sit at the table, and it might be a good idea to allow them to leave the table when they have finished Let children eat at their own pace.

Some children cause anxiety because they may:

- refuse to eat many foods
- take a long time to eat their food
- refuse to swallow food
- display other poor eating behaviours.

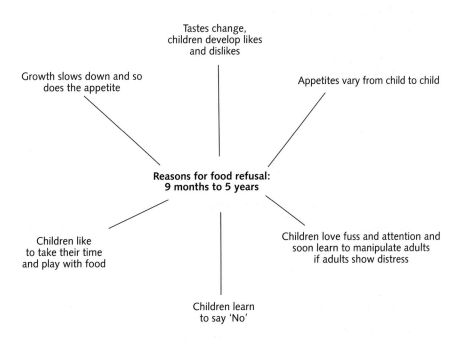

Food refusal – 9 months to 5 years

If a child is causing anxiety, make a record of what food is being refused, how she behaves at the table, such as crying, complaining or throwing food, and what food she enjoys. You may see a pattern, such as too many snacks prior to the meal, and may be able to resolve the problem. This must be discussed with the parents.

There is a fashion today for some parents to allow their children to 'graze'. This means eating continually, on demand, and usually walking around with the food. Most nannies will not be happy with this, and it will have to be discussed with the parents.

GOOD PRACTICE IN ENCOURAGING HEALTHY EATING HABITS

1   Let children help themselves to food at the table.
2   Allow children to help prepare food sometimes.
3   Encourage children to set the table and clear away food afterwards.
4   Talk to children during the meal about the foods.
5   Don't make a fuss about accidents at the table, and let children help mop up the spills.
6   Present food in an interesting way, mixing colours, flavours and textures.
7   Make the table look attractive, with a clean cloth and perhaps a small jug of flowers.
8   Encourage children to try new foods, presenting one new food at a time, when they are not tired or ill.
9   Set a good example by sitting at the table with the children and showing your enjoyment of the food.

Domestic routines

You will find life easier if you develop routines to manage the domestic chores that go with the job of being a nanny. For example, in a family where you are caring for a school-age child, a pre-schooler and a baby you will need every day to:

■   get yourself up and have a shower
■   wash, dress and feed the baby
■   wake up the children and help them dress if help is needed
■   prepare and supervise breakfast
■   make up lunch boxes
■   take children to pre-school and school
■   wash up the breakfast things
■   make beds and tidy rooms
■   put on the washing machine
■   feed the baby
■   sterilise feeding equipment
■   fold up and put away clean and dry washing
■   collect children at end of nursery and school day
■   feed the baby

- make tea and clear up the dishes
- supervise homework
- help the children care for their pets
- provide stimulating indoor and outdoor activities for all the children
- feed and bath the baby and put her to bed
- bath and prepare the older children for bed
- wash the baby's toys
- lay out the clothes for the following day
- record your observations and keep your daily diary up to date
- have time with the parents to discuss the day.

Several times a week you will:
- take children to after-school activities
- iron clothes where strictly necessary, such as school shirts
- do the shopping
- repair children's clothes and sew in labels
- mend any broken toys and wash any that have become dirty.

Once a week you will:
- change the children's and your own bed linen
- clean all the children's rooms thoroughly
- wash the children's and your towels
- take the children to the library
- plan menus for the following week.

From time to time you will:
- arrange appointments and accompany children to the health clinic, dentist, optician, GP and so on
- prepare clothes and pack for holidays
- check all the safety equipment, such as the high chair, harness and car restraints
- research new equipment
- try on clothes for summer/winter and replace any that the children have grown out of
- buy new shoes
- take children to have their hair cut
- arrange birthday parties.

The above lists looks terrifying, but it will be helpful in a new job to make sure that you are managing your time as usefully as possible. Remember to leave time to play with the baby in between chores. The list will change as the children grow older and you will have encouraged them to become more independent and take on some of the chores for themselves.

Holidays with the family

It sounds exciting to take a job with a family that travels abroad quite often, with you sharing the holiday. It does not always work out as you would imagine. It is necessary to have lengthy discussions with the family, to find out exactly what they expect from you when they are on holiday with you and the children.

Some employers might presume that the holiday is part of your annual leave, and this is certainly not the case. In fact, you might have to work harder than you would at home.

CASE STUDY

Rachel, a daily nanny, had been working happily for a family for a year when they asked her to accompany them on a holiday to Corfu. She had never been abroad before so she was looking forward to a holiday in the sun and spending fun time with the children on a sunny beach. She hoped to teach the two older ones to swim, as she held a swimming teacher's certificate.

The holiday was not as she anticipated. The two-year-old hated the feel of sand on his feet and screamed every time they went on the beach. The baby developed a stomach upset, and had to stay out of the sun for a few days. The parents expected her to look after the children all day and every evening, while they visited local sights and restaurants. She had her meals alone in her bedroom, while keeping an eye on the children. She was not expected to have any time off, as the parents seemed to presume that paying for her to come on holiday would result in her happily offering twenty-four hour care. She managed to negotiate one morning and one evening off during the fortnight, but felt the parents resented this.

1 How might this situation have been avoided?
2 Was there anything Rachel could have said or done during the holiday to show how she was feeling?
3 Could Rachel have prepared the children for the holiday in any way?

Good preparation is the key for a successful and happy holiday for everyone. When the idea is first raised, sit down with the parents and sort out the following issues.

1 What are your exact duties during the holiday?
2 What hours will you be expected to work?
3 How much free time will you have?
4 Will you eat with the family in the evening?
5 Will you have your own room or be expected to share with the children?
6 Will there be any additional costs for you?
7 Is the family clear that this is not part of your annual leave?

Having agreed these issues with the parents, assure them that you will continue to meet your professional responsibilities towards them and the children. Part of your duties will entail planning and preparing for the children. This would include the following.

■ Check with the parents that passports, immunisations and travel insurance are up to date. Remember to check yours as well.
■ Check whether all the equipment the children might need, such as high chairs, car seats and cots will be available.

- Check what facilities there will be for washing and ironing clothes.
- Be aware that the environment will be potentially hazardous (swimming pools, the sea, insects and so on).
- Make up a bag of snacks, drinks and amusements for the children to help them during the journey. Include wet wipes!

The parents will probably expect you to pack for the children. You will need to make sure that their holiday clothes still fit them, and shop for new ones where necessary. The child's suitcase is likely to contain:

- clothes suitable for the climate: hats, gloves and warm shoes for the cold, baggy cotton tee-shirts and sun hats for the heat
- maximum sun-factor protection cream
- plastic sandals for the beach
- a First Aid kit, containing child paracetamol, a thermometer, cream for bites and stings, antiseptic cream, insect repellent, waterproof plasters, rehydration sachets for diarrhoea
- safety reins and swimming armbands
- some favourite foods, such as cereals
- disposal bibs
- a portable potty
- wet wipes and nappies

- favourite toys
- comfort objects.

When you arrive at the holiday resort, be prepared for the children being tired and grumpy after the journey. It may take a day or two for them to adjust to the new environment. Being out of their normal routine can be disturbing for some children, so try to establish a sensible holiday routine, with meals and bed-times as much near the normal times as is feasible.

Some places that you might visit with the family might present a threat to the children's health and safety.

GOOD PRACTICE IN KEEPING CHILDREN HEALTHY AND SAFE ON HOLIDAY

1. Make sure the drinking water is safe. If unsure, use bottled water even for clean-ing teeth. Avoid ice in drinks and make sure that the bottled water is sealed and the cans unopened. Salads should be avoided in some countries.
2. Check that the local milk is pasteurised.
3. Make sure that the children drink frequently to prevent dehydration.
4. Rub sun cream into the child's skin before going outside using a high-protection factor. Re-apply every two hours and after swimming.
5. If the sun is too hot in the middle of the day, stay indoors from 11 am until 3 pm.
6. Keep the children covered in hats and tee-shirts and encourage them to wear plastic shoes on the beach to protect their feet.
7. Be very watchful of the children near the sea or in the swimming pool.

5 KEEPING CHILDREN SAFE AND HEALTHY

> **This chapter includes:**
> - **Accidents**
> - **Checking hazards inside and outside the home**
> - **Dealing with emergencies**
> - **Hygiene and the prevention of infection**
> - **Medication**
> - **Child protection**

As a nanny, you will have become aware of the need to provide a hazard-free and safe environment in the home that allows children to explore safely, and in turn aids all their areas of development and promotes independence. It is not always easy to find the balance between allowing too much independence and being over-protective. The younger the child, the more supervision is necessary.

Children are the responsibility of the adults who care for them. An accident is something that happens that is not anticipated or foreseen, and may be preventable with care and thought. Sometimes accidents occur because the carer is in a hurry, is experiencing stress due to personal problems, or is feeling tired and therefore less alert. It is obviously essential that you hold personal liability insurance.

Accidents

The latest figures from the Royal Society for the Prevention of Accidents (ROSPA) and the Home Accident Surveillance System (HASS) show that the most serious accidents happen in the kitchen and on the stairs, and the largest number of accidents happens in the living room/dining room area. Forty per cent of all fatal accidents happen at home. Most accidents occur between 6 and 7 pm.

One child in twelve will be treated for a home accident each year. Half the children are under four years of age. Boys are more likely to have an accident than girls. Children in lower socio-economic groups are more likely to have a fatal accident than those in higher groups. Factors, such as divorce, death in the family, chronic illness, homelessness and moving home increase the likelihood of a child having an accident, due to the stress caused to the main carer.

To prevent accidents to children, a combination of factors is required:
- improvements in the planning, design and manufacture of products, to create a safer environment
- an increasing awareness of risks, hazards and safety equipment
- education and training to improve knowledge and skills.

Safety equipment can include:

- radiator guards
- low-surface-temperature radiators
- tap covers
- bath thermometers
- baby bath supports
- protectors to cover sharp corners
- video locks
- socket covers
- fire guards
- smoke alarms
- curtain cords control kits
- stair gates
- flexible tubing to hold electric wires
- door slam protectors
- door gates
- rug grips
- cupboard and fridge safety locks
- window locks
- window bars
- oven guards
- short coiled flexes
- harnesses and restraints.

A professional approach to safety might involve you in carrying out the following checks on a regular basis.

■ Examine each room of the house for obvious hazards.
■ Test and maintain all safety equipment.
■ Make sure that all the children's equipment, such as high chairs, pushchairs and prams are clean, have attached harnesses, and are well maintained.
■ Make sure the garden is safe.
■ Request that the car is regularly serviced, and has appropriate restraints and car seats fitted.

Checking hazards inside and outside the home

Keeping the children safe is not just a matter of checking for hazards, and being sure that there is nothing dangerous around. It entails constant vigilance and imagination whilst inspecting and maintaining all equipment on a daily basis.

1 Check domestic and play equipment regularly for sharp edges, splinters, and loose pieces. Do not give children under three small playthings, such as marbles or small Lego™ pieces.

2 Keep the following objects out of sight and out of reach of children:
■ medicines and tablets, which must be kept locked in a high cupboard
■ matches
■ sharp objects, such as knives and razor blades
■ plastic bags
■ household cleaners and chemicals
■ alcohol
■ cigarettes.

3 Ensure that safety gates for stairs or doorways are secure.

4 Never use baby walkers as there have been serious accidents when using this equipment.

5 Do not use pillows for any child under eighteen months. Use a firm mattress with no gaps between it and the cot.

6 Always supervise children in the kitchen where there are many hazards. You must be sure to:
■ turn saucepan handles away from the edge of the stove
■ keep all hot and sharp objects away from the edge of units
■ use short, coiled flexes on electrical equipment
■ have a fire blanket, and know how to use it
■ keep chest freezers locked
■ keep the doors to washing machines and tumble dryers shut
■ avoid using tablecloths that hang down
■ use a harness fitted to the high chair and see that it is always secured
■ always supervise children when they are eating or drinking and never leave a baby propped up with a bottle.

7 Avoid giving nuts or boiled sweets to children.

8 Try to keep floor space free of obstruction, as much as possible.

9 Make sure cords are not trailing from curtains or blinds.

10 Avoid anything around babies' necks, such as anorak strings, dummies on strings, and ribbons on hats.

11 Fit child-resistant locks on all windows, keeping keys readily available in case of fire.

12 Highlight large glass doors with stickers.

13 Secure doors leading to a cellar, balcony and any unsupervised outside area.

14 Do not leave a hot drink unattended, and never sit a child on your lap while you drink something hot.

TO PREVENT FIRE

■ Make sure all fires have securely fitted safety guards.
■ Encourage parents to have the water-heating and heating equipment regularly inspected and maintained.

- Encourage parents to have smoke alarms fitted and keep them maintained.
- Plan how you and the children would escape from the house, particularly if there are sealed windows or permanently locked doors.

TO PREVENT ELECTRIC SHOCKS

- Ask your family to cover all power points with child-resistant socket covers.
- Check all flexes regularly for fraying and ask your family to replace those that are worn.
- Ask your family not to put electrical appliances in the bathroom.
- Ask your family to make sure new electric appliances come fitted with a plug.

GOOD PRACTICE IN THE GARDEN

1 Keep garage and shed doors locked, and keep all equipment and materials locked away out of sight and out of reach of children.
2 Secure garden gates and fences so that children cannot get out and people and animals cannot get in.
3 Cover or fence-off any area of equipment containing water.
4 Cover sand pits when not in use to avoid soiling by animals.
5 Identify and protect children from poisonous plants.
6 Check all outdoor play equipment such as slides and climbing frames regularly for safety, and make sure that any new equipment is correctly installed, and that the space underneath either has mats or wood chippings to ensure a soft landing.
7 Avoid trailing clothes lines.
8 Supervise animals when children are in the garden, and put a cat net over a baby's pram.
9 It is safest to avoid ponds and water butts in gardens, but be aware that a young child can drown in two inches of water.

Activity
1 You are caring for a six-month old baby and an active four-year old. Which hazards in the house and in the garden are particularly dangerous for each age group?
2 Devise a safety check list for the home and garden.
3 Identify indoor and outdoor plants that might be poisonous.

AWAY FROM HOME

You will be taking children out very often, going shopping, posting letters, collecting older children from school, visiting libraries and friends. You may find yourself having to manage a baby in a pushchair and an active toddler.

With very young children, it is prudent to avoid places where:
- there are very large open spaces and a child might wander off
- there is a lot of traffic and pollution
- animal droppings are not cleared up promptly
- there is a great deal of litter dropped, such as in some markets
- the children have to be quiet and keep still for a long time
- it is difficult to supervise more than one child safely, such as in a playground with swings, high obstacle courses and slides, and unsupervised water play
- there are sand pits that are not covered at night to prevent animals from fouling them.

It is a good idea to take a small emergency First Aid kit on any outing. This might contain antiseptic wipes, antiseptic cream, plasters, antihistamine cream, medicated tissues and an ice pack. It is never too early to start teaching children the basic rules of safety, and making sure that they know their address and home telephone number. When in parks and on beaches, always identify a highly visible point, such as a café, where children should go if they become temporarily separated.

GOOD PRACTICE WHEN TAKING THE CHILDREN OUT

1 Maintain prams and pushchairs in good working order and check brakes regularly.
2 Fit harnesses to prams and pushchairs and always use them.
3 Be a good role model when crossing the road, teaching children road safety from an early age. Always use zebra or pelican crossings if available. Make sure children are either holding your hand, or the pram.
4 Never push the pram or other conveyance into the road first, so as to stop the traffic.
5 Be alert when in shopping centres and other busy areas. Use personal restraints, such as harnesses or reins.
6 When in a park, use the 'children only' areas and exercise constant supervision in the playground.
7 If you are taking children further afield, you will need to plan the trip carefully and well in advance. Consultation with parents is essential.
8 Children should never be left alone outside shops or schools. Prams must either be taken into shops with you, or you must carry the baby.

Activity

Plan a picnic in your local park, with children aged one year, three years and six years.

What would it be essential to have with you so as to make sure the children were protected and you are prepared for any emergency?

GOOD PRACTICE WHEN USING THE CAR

You might find yourself driving a car to transport the children from place to place. There are certain checks you need to make, and rules to establish.

1 Check that the car insurance is valid and fully comprehensive.
2 All adults in the car must wear seat belts in the front and in the back.
3 All children in the car should be secured in child restraints appropriate to the size of the child, with the younger children in the back.
4 Make sure that child locks are activated when you have the children with you.
5 Try not to have the family pet in the car when you are transporting children.
6 All child restraints should be professionally fitted.
7 Never allow the children to stand up on the seats, between the front seats, or travel in the back section of an estate or hatchback.
8 Make sure that children alight on to the pavement, and not the road.
9 Make sure that all the children are properly secured in the car before you get in.
10 Be a careful and alert driver, a good example to the children.

Always be alert to danger, and aware that children are small vulnerable beings. Your knowledge of children's development should allow you to anticipate some potential hazards and risks, and understanding the children's personalities will help you to predict how they will react to situations. Part of your role is to teach children about dangers, and how to protect themselves.

A United Nations survey, published in February 2001, showed that the UK has one of the lowest rates of child deaths caused by accidents and abuse. The survey points out that this good safety record may have a down side in that children are no longer being allowed to explore their boundaries and develop their own sense of risk and danger.

CASE STUDY

In the Easter holidays, Anita, a newly employed nanny, took her two children to the Zoo with her friend Jessie, a nanny who looks after three children. They had to take two cars. All the children were playing up, wanting to sit in particular seats next to friends. When they met up at the ticket office, Anita was horrified to find that Jamie, who is seven, was not with them. Anita thought he had gone with Jessie, and she thought he was with Anita.

The day was ruined, as they all had to return home, to find Jamie in tears in the back garden.

1 What could Anita have done to prevent this situation happening?
2 How would you have dealt with Jamie?
3 What would you say to Jamie's parents?

Dealing with emergencies

There are many types of emergencies that might arise during the day and you need to be prepared. An emergency may involve a child:
- losing consciousness
- experiencing heavy blood loss, such as a serious nose bleed
- breaking a bone
- having difficulty in breathing, maybe having an asthma attack
- falling on broken glass, causing a deep wound.

To cope with any emergency you should:
- remain calm
- provide First Aid, without putting yourself or other children in danger
- not provide food or drink.

You should call an ambulance and not move the child if:
- you think she has hurt her back or neck or have any injury that may be made worse by moving her
- the child is in shock and needs your constant attention
- the child has severe chest pain or difficulty in breathing
- you should have with you a medical and emergency information chart, as shown in Chapter 3, page 35.

When you completed the chart with the parents, it was an opportunity to discuss how you handle any specific crisis. For example, if a child is prone to asthma, some parents might wish the child to be taken straight to hospital and meet you there while others might like to come to you from work. A mobile phone could be an asset, if there was an emergency where you were out with the children.

It is sensible to enrol on a First Aid course, if you do not already hold the certificate. Those with expertise, such as the St John Ambulance or the British Red Cross, teach the courses. All First Aid certificates need to be up-dated regularly. First Aid is the immediate action taken to treat a person who has been injured or has suddenly become ill. Knowing what to do can save life and prevent further injury, but it is important to know your limits and do only what you are competent to do. Urgent care requires you to:

■ remove the victim from the source of danger
■ check breathing and give artificial respiration if necessary
■ control bleeding
■ place the child in the recovery position if she is unconscious
■ call for help, giving accurate information, and keeping any substance that might be relevant to diagnosing the condition.

Many hospitals now offer two-hour resuscitation sessions, which you might like to attend, prior to taking a full First Aid course.

Many accidents cause shock in children, and you will need to recognise the signs, which are:

■ pale cold sweaty skin
■ rapid pulse, becoming weaker
■ shallow fast breathing
■ restlessness, yawning and sighing
■ thirst
■ loss of consciousness.

If you think one of the children is suffering from shock, you should summon medical aid.

The parents should provide you with a First Aid box.

Hygiene and the prevention of infection

It is particularly important for nannies to have high standards of personal hygiene, as you will have to carry out intimate tasks for the children, as well as teaching them the rules of hygiene.

Infection is spread by touch, food and water, animals, droplets in the air and through cuts and grazes. All children are vulnerable to infection and it is important that you understand how disease is transmitted in order to minimise children's exposure to bacterial, fungal and viral infections. The rooms that harbour most germs are the kitchen and the bathroom and, as you will be having other children using these, they need to be scrupulously clean.

GOOD PRACTICE IN THE PREVENTION OF INFECTION

1 Make sure that you and the children wash your hands after using the lavatory, handling animals and their equipment, coughing or sneezing, and before eating. In addition, you need to wash thoroughly after changing nappies, wiping noses, wiping bottoms and handling raw food.
2 Keep the kitchen working surfaces, utensils and implements clean.
3 Always keep food covered that is left out on the working surface.
4 Never re-freeze food that has already been defrosted.
5 Never store raw meat alongside other food. Keep it well wrapped at the bottom of the refrigerator.
6 Do not allow the refrigerator to become over-crowded, as this will impede the circulation of air.
7 Meat and fish should never be eaten after they have been refrigerated for more than three days.
8 Make sure the refrigerator is no more than 5 degrees centigrade. The freezer should be set at minus 18 degrees centigrade to prevent bacteria multiplying.
9 Feeding bottles and teats need to be sterilised for as long as they are used, as milk is an excellent medium for bacteria.
10 Keep rubbish bins covered and scrupulously clean.
11 Keep animals out of the kitchen.

Activity

1 Suggest two hygiene routines that will help to prevent infection.
2 Describe how you dispose of waste products and soiled items hygienically and safely.

Keeping a clean home will prevent germs from multiplying. The use of soap and water, fresh air and sunlight will destroy many germs. Using chemical disinfectants, such as carbolic or strong bleach, will destroy germs but are potentially harmful to children and pets, and need to be locked away. Antiseptics are weak disinfectants that prevent the growth of organisms but do not destroy them. They can be equally dangerous to children.

Those keeping any kind of pet should know about its food and habits, and how to care for them.

GOOD PRACTICE IN CARING FOR PETS

1 Children should be taught the importance of looking after animals, feeding them and cleaning out cages.
2 They must be told the importance of washing hands after handling a pet or cleaning a cage.
3 Children should be discouraged from kissing pets or letting pets lick their faces.
4 Sick animals must always be seen by a vet.
5 Disinfectant should be used to wash floors soiled with animal excreta.

6 Animals' foods and plates should be kept and washed separately from those used by humans.

7 Puppies and kittens should be wormed when very young, and before this, children should not handle them. They should be wormed again at regular intervals.

8 No family should have a pet that is not tolerant of young children.

9 All animals need space and exercise and a person who is devoted to their care.

10 If you are not sure how to care for a pet, ask the parents to buy an up-to-date handbook, outlining the basic care procedures.

11 Be aware that the arrival of a new baby in the home may seem threatening to the family pet. Do not leave them alone together until you are sure the pet has accepted the baby.

Activity
Investigate two diseases that are associated with pets. What action would you take to ensure that the children in your care are not put at risk by their pets?

Medication

Some children require routine medication for a chronic condition. For example, a child might suffer from asthma, and would need some form of inhaler to prevent attacks, as well as a medicine to have at hand if she should become ill. Other children might require medication for a sudden acute condition, such as an ear infection or tonsillitis. Before agreeing to give any medication, you should discuss it very carefully with the parents. For some medical conditions, such as asthma, you may require training in how to give the medication. It is sensible to ask for signed consent from the parents before agreeing to administer any medication. Be very clear about the dosage and the timing and keep a written record of any medicine that you have administered. This would also apply to any accident that one of the children might have. Keeping a clear record will not only be helpful if the child should become worse, but will also protect you from any allegations of neglect.

All medicines should be stored in the original container and be properly labelled. They must be in a secure place, out of the reach of children. Most medicines should be kept in a cool dry environment, and out of sunlight. Many medicines need refrigeration and should be kept in a secure box, separate from food, and labelled 'Medicines'. You should not prescribe medication yourself, not even paracetamol for a raised temperature. If you become concerned, you should contact the parents immediately.

Child protection

These days, there is a great deal in the media about abused and neglected children and, while we must be careful not to over-protect children, we must always be alert to the dangers surrounding them. It is rare, but not unknown, for nannies to have major concerns about abuse and neglect within the family they are employed to work with. Some nannies might feel that the children are emotionally neglected because the parents work full time, and they can find little time to spend with the children.

Most abuse is perpetrated by people known to the child, close family or family friends. The media has aroused people's anxieties about stranger abuse, yet the amount of abuse by strangers is a tiny percentage. Abuse happens in all socio-economic groups and across all cultural, religious and ethnic groups. Both boys and girls are abused by both men and women.

RECOGNITION OF ABUSE AND NEGLECT

As a person who cares for children in a professional manner, you need to be able to recognise the signs of abuse and neglect. Whatever sort of relationship you may have made with the family, your first duty is to the child.

Shaking babies and children

Shaking a child can cause serious injury, even death, and many people are ignorant of the effects of such shaking. Violent shaking of a young baby has the same effect on the baby's brain as dropping her directly onto a concrete floor. A baby's head is large compared to the rest of her body and the neck muscles are not yet strong enough to support it. Shaking the head with great force will cause tiny blood vessels to tear and bleed inside the brain. This can lead to loss of vision and hearing, fits, brain damage or death. Serious harm to older children can also be caused by shaking.

Most children will suffer accidental injuries. Deciding what is accidental and what has been inflicted upon a child can be a very difficult process, testing the skills of experienced paediatricians. Many signs that might lead you to think that abuse has taken place, might be explained. For example, bald patches might occur if a child frequently pulls and twists her hair as a comfort habit.

SEXUAL ABUSE

Sexual abuse ranges from showing pornographic materials or inappropriate touching to penetration, rape and incest. It is found in all cultures, all classes and in all religious groups. It may involve very young babies. It often begins gradually and increases over a period of time. Children are trusting and dependent, wanting to please and gain love and approval.

The majority of sexually abused children know the perpetrator who is often a member of the family, a close family friend or someone in a position of trust. It rarely involves the use of physical force and there are usually no physical signs, but if you did see bruising in the genital area, blood stains, torn underclothing or vaginal discharge, you would be immediately alerted and take steps to protect the child.

CHANGES IN BEHAVIOUR

Abuse and neglect may cause a change of behaviour that will vary a great deal according to the age of the child. Some areas of abuse are more difficult to recognise than physical abuse and neglect. For example, emotional abuse, such as constantly belittling and undermining the child in everything she does, can be almost as damaging as physical abuse. An indication that this is going on may appear in the behaviour of the child

In addition to more generalised changes in behaviour a child suffering from sexual abuse might:

■ behave in a way sexually inappropriate to her age, particularly when involved in imaginary play
■ produce drawings of sex organs and use sexual language
■ display insecurity and cling to trusted adults
■ act in a placatory or flirtatious way, or in an inappropriately mature manner.

Changes in behaviour are not necessarily due to abuse or neglect. Children go through many difficult stages in their normal development. It is only when there is a cluster of behavioural changes that you should begin to consider the possibility of abuse.

Activity
List the ways in which you might recognise distress in children.

DISCLOSURE

If you find yourself in a position where an older child is disclosing abuse to you, you need to respond in a way that will not further harm the child. Listen carefully and patiently, without asking leading questions; that is, without putting words into the child's mouth, or making them give the response you want them to. You should:

■ attempt to make the child feel secure and safe when disclosing to you
■ reassure the child, stating that you are pleased to have been told and that you believe her
■ never look shocked or disbelieving
■ never express criticism of the perpetrator
■ never promise to take an action, which you may not be able to carry out
■ reassure the child that she is not to blame for the abuse
■ explain that in order to help her, you will have to tell other people what is happening
■ keep calm
■ resist pressing for information or questioning the child
■ make an immediate timed, dated and signed record of the conversation.

This is an intimidating situation to find yourself in, and you may find it difficult to know how to proceed. Common reasons for not taking action are:

■ disbelief
■ fear of being seen as interfering

- fear of becoming involved in a difficult or distressing situation
- friendship and loyalty to the parents
- fear that the family will be split up and the children taken away
- fear of losing your job.

You have a professional responsibility to protect the children and to stop any abuse that you think may be taking place. If you are concerned about a child, her parents may be the first people to talk to. If there is a satisfactory explanation it will avoid unnecessary investigations.

You may consider the possibility that you will be deceived by the parents or vulnerable if the parents accuse you to protect themselves. They may also refuse to believe that a close relative or friend of the family has abused a child.

If you feel a child is at risk and you are a member of PANN, they will offer support and advice and put you in touch with a local solicitor within 24 hours. The police and/or social services may have to be involved, and you will be supported by PANN at this time.

CASE STUDY

Sally is two and a half, and has been cared for by you for six months on a daily basis. The family is affluent, living in a large detached house. Sally's father is frequently away from home, and Jane, her mother, works full time. It has been difficult to establish a relationship with Jane. She seems to have very little time for or patience with Sally, often describing her in a disparaging manner. Sally is becoming quieter and more withdrawn, and on one occasion said she had been shut in a cupboard for a long time. When Jane arrives home one day, she looks tearful, upset and smells of drink. Sally runs and clings to Jane who pushes her away.

1 What factors might cause you concern?
2 How might her mother's rejection affect Sally's emotional development?
3 What are Sally's needs and what are the family's needs?
4 What might you do to help Sally and her family?

HOW TO PROTECT YOURSELF FROM ALLEGATIONS OF ABUSE

When working as a nanny you need to be aware that you are in a vulnerable situation. There have been some cases of nannies being accused of abuse so make sure your behaviour is professional at all times and open to scrutiny. There are steps you can take to prevent yourself being unjustly accused of abuse. These include:

- keeping a record of all accidents and incidents involving the children in your care and keeping the parents informed of any incidents, accidents or events that have occurred during the day
- making a note of the incident if another adult witnesses an accident to one of the children
- keeping a written record if you are suspicious or concerned about a child

- joining PANN and any local support group
- making a note of any injuries, however minor, sustained by a child when not in your care
- ensuring the children are well supervised at all times, and not leaving them in the care of unauthorised people
- telling the parents and recording the incident if a child behaves in a sexually inappropriate manner towards you
- encouraging independence in children, and not carrying out intimate tasks that they are quite capable of doing for themselves
- not asking children to keep secrets
- never trying to manage children's challenging behaviour by handling a child roughly
- never shaking, hitting or smacking a child in your care, even if the parents want to give their permission
- not shouting or using a sarcastic approach with children
- using appropriate language in front of children
- never forcing kisses and cuddles on children who do not wish it while responding to children's emotional needs
- taking advantage of any child protection training courses
- not allowing children to come into your bed at any time.

If a complaint is made against you, you will feel distressed and most unhappy. Keep a record of all conversations you have, both face to face and on the telephone, concerning this matter. Include times, dates, places and participants. Keep copies of all correspondence. You should seek legal advice, either independently or through PANN (if you are a member), who will put you in touch with a local solicitor within twenty-four hours.

SURVEILLANCE

In some countries, surveillance by hidden cameras and the employment of private detectives to find out what the nanny is doing in her time off has become more common. These practices are usually employed by wealthy families who fear that their children may be kidnapped.

In the UK, the latest form of surveillance to be developed uses the Internet to link parents to their children during the day. Using a password-controlled system, the parents can connect to cameras installed in the room where their children are playing and observe what they are up to. Although restricted almost exclusively to a few daycare establishments at present, this form of surveillance is likely to increase in popularity for use in family homes.

In general, it is important to remember that although there may be a place for using a camera with your co-operation to enable the parents to keep in touch with what the children are doing, to use a camera secretly to spy on you is a breach of trust.

It is very rare for a nanny to abuse or neglect a child in her care. Such cases always attract the widest media coverage, and so one supposes that it occurs more often than it does.

PARENTAL CONFLICT

If you work for parents who are separated and are in dispute about arrangements for the care and responsibility of the children, the parent with custody may have taken legal advice on how to protect the children from the possibility of abduction. During this decade, the figures for the abduction of children have risen dramatically, so much so that the UK government has decided that all children born from October 1998 onwards should have their own passport and not share that of their parent.

Your employer will have discussed any fears she might have during the interview, but once you are employed you must make sure that you are quite clear on any arrangements for access days, collection from school or areas of conflict.

Some of the families you work for will be demonstrative and show affection by frequent kissing and cuddling, while other families may be equally fond of their children but are not very outgoing with their emotions. You will need to build up a trusting relationship with the family and this will happen only with time. All children should feel they can come to you for help and protection. It is important to discuss this matter with the parents, as the message must be consistent.

6 CARING FOR THE SICK CHILD

> ## This chapter includes:
> - **Recognition of illness**
> - **Caring for children who are unwell**
> - **Infection**
> - **Minor ailments**
> - **Infestations**
> - **Chronic medical conditions**

To make sure that the children in your care are healthy, you will be working in partnership with their parents. A nanny can be regarded to some extent as a health educator who wishes to promote the health of children by understanding health issues and setting a good example. You will need to understand the importance of routine health surveillance and screening programmes, and be aware of the facilities of the local health clinic.

From time to time, all children become sick. It is probable that you will have to look after children with coughs and colds, minor childhood illnesses such as chickenpox and infestations such as head lice. With your training you should be able to meet the needs of sick children.

You may be caring for chronically ill children, who need regular routine care and medication. A child who has a condition such as asthma or diabetes will need careful monitoring to achieve optimum health.

Recognition of illness

Despite modern immunisation programmes, a few infectious diseases remain in circulation. As you get to know the children and understand how they behave and react to situations, you will soon learn when they are sickening for something and the chart on page 78 may help you to recognise the signs and symptoms of common infections, and indicate the care that should be given.

If you are caring for a small baby, it is very important that you are alert to the signs and symptoms of ill health. You must contact the parents and seek medical advice immediately if the baby shows signs of:
- being a very quiet pale baby, difficult to rouse and refusing to feed
- vomiting and diarrhoea
- crying and refusing to be comforted
- noisy or laboured breathing
- convulsions or fits

Common childhood infections

Illness	Incubation	Signs and symptoms	Care	Immunisation available
Chickenpox	14–21 days	Raised temperature Malaise Small red spots – blisters – scabs Skin irritation	Extra fluids Light diet Tepid baths with bicarbonate of soda Loose clothes Calamine lotion Keep fingernails short	None

Measles	8–15 days	Cough and cold
		Raised temperature
		Sore eyes
		Blotchy red rash, starts behind
		  ears, spreads down the body
		White koplicks spots on inside
		  of cheeks
			Seek GP advice
			Rest
			Fluids
			Light diet
			Tepid sponging
			Watch for ear infection
			Keep mouth clean
			Darkened room?
			Eye drops
				Yes

Gastroenteritis	Variable	Unwell
		Severe vomiting and diarrhoea
		Possible signs of dehydration,
		  dry mouth and skin, less urine,
		  sunken anterior fontanelle in
		  small babies
			Seek GP advice
			Keep cool and
			  comfortable
			Give extra fluids or oral
			  rehydration solution if
			  prescribed.
			Skin and mouth care
				No

Meningitis (bacterial or viral)	Variable	Raised temperature
		Severe headache
		Vomiting
		Stiff, painful neck
		Confusion
		Dislike of light
		Irritability
		Rash with meningococcal
		  meningitis
			**URGENT MEDICAL
			  ATTENTION**
			Treatment and
			  care in hospital
				Yes for HIB type and meningitis C

Mumps	12–24 days	Malaise
		Pain and tenderness around
		  ear and jaw
		Swelling on either or both
		  sides of jaw
		Raised temperature
			Keep comfortable
			Liquid diet
			Extra fluids (use straw)
			Analgesic
			Rest
				Yes

Rubella (German measles)	12–21 days	Mild cold and fever
		Rash of flat spots on face and
		  perhaps the body
		May have swollen glands at the
		  back of the neck
			Extra fluids
			Keep away from
			  pregnant women
				Yes

Scarlet fever	2–5 days	Raised temperature
		Severe sore throat with
		  white patches
		Tongue looks red
		Scarlet rash on face,
		  spreading to body
			Seek GP advice
			Extra fluids
			Rest
			Antibiotics
			Light diet
			Observe for complications,
			  such as ear and kidney
			  infections
				No

Whooping cough	7–14 days	Raised temperature
		Cough and cold at start, cough
		  getting worse
		Characteristic continuous coughing
		  and choking, may vomit or find
		  it hard to breathe
		Can last for weeks
			Seek GP advice
			Antibiotics
			Rest and reassurance
			Extra fluids
			Give food and drink after
			  coughing bouts
			Watch for complications
				Yes

- rash
- persistent cough
- discharge from the ears, or obvious discomfort in the ears, shown by the baby pulling her ear
- changes in the stool or urine
- lethargy and pallor
- sunken anterior fontanelle (soft spot on top of head), indicating dehydration
- bulging anterior fontanelle, indicating pressure in the skull, for which seek immediate medical advice.

When you have been working for the family for a while, the parents will trust you enough to allow you to contact the doctor or emergency services yourself, especially if it is difficult for you to get in touch with the parents quickly. With small babies, fast action can save a life. When you contact the doctor or emergency services, you should offer accurate information. You can help parents by remaining calm, and reassuring them that appropriate action has been taken, as you will appreciate how concerned they are.

In addition to the common childhood complaints, there are other infections of which you must be aware. The most important of these is meningitis, which can develop within hours into a life-threatening illness. The signs and symptoms are variable, which makes both the viral and the bacterial forms of this infection so difficult to diagnose. These will include:

- vomiting
- headache
- high temperature
- stiff neck
- joint pains
- drowsiness or confusion
- dislike of bright lights
- rash of red/purple spots or bruises that do not fade when pressed with a glass. Medical aid should be sought urgently.

Caring for children who are unwell

Sick babies and children need to be with someone that they know and trust. It could be you, or you may be sharing the care with the child's parents. If this is the case, you will need to agree on the routines, understand and agree on the giving of medication, and work out a rota so that you can all get some rest.

If the child's temperature suddenly rises, it is important to take action so as to prevent a convulsion. The child needs to get rid of excess heat, so keep the room cool and airy, remove excess clothing and bedding, and give frequent drinks of water. Sponging with lukewarm water may help to reduce the temperature. You may have discussed the possibility of this situation with the parents, and have their permission to administer paracetamol.

GIVING MEDICATION

You should never administer medication to a child unless you have the permission of the parents. With any prescribed medicine it is essential to know:

■ when to take it, and for how long
■ what the medicine should do
■ how long it will take to work, and how you can tell it is working
■ what to do if it does not seem to be working
■ what to do if you forget a dose
■ what are the possible side-effects.

Most medicines for children are in liquid form. Shake the bottle thoroughly before giving a dose. Tablets are more concentrated than liquid medicines, and may need to be crushed to a powder. Slow-release and coated tablets must be swallowed whole. Eye, ear and nose drops are designed to coat the affected surface.

When giving medicine, it is a good idea to sit the child on your lap and have a towel and damp cloth handy in case of spills. Measure the medicine into a non-spill tube spoon. Gradually tip the medicine in to the back of the cheek. Chase it down with a favourite drink. Never mix medicines into a drink or bottle.

As soon as you have given the medication, record it on a piece of paper, with the date and time and amount. You should do this, even if you have been unsuccessful in administering the full amount, indicating the difficulty, especially if you are sharing the care with the parents or another nanny. All medicines should be stored in the original container and be properly labelled. They must be kept in a secure place, out of the reach of children. Most medicines should be kept in cool, dry conditions and out of sunlight. Medicines needing refrigeration should be kept in a secure plastic box separate from food.

NURSING CARE

There are very few conditions that require children to remain in bed, isolated from the rest of the family. The house should be warm and well-ventilated and children allowed to rest on the sofa, perhaps covered with a light blanket. Bright lights would be irritating to most children who are ill, as would loud noises.

Children who are sick should be offered regular fluids (not fizzy drinks) and given a light diet. If the child refuses food, it does not matter, but it is important that she is encouraged to drink. A child with a fever may become sweaty and uncomfortable, and will need to be helped to wash. Her hair should be tied back loosely and brushed regularly.

An irritable rash will be soothed by a warm bath with soda bicarbonate added to the water. Her mouth will need to kept fresh, either by cleaning her teeth or encouraging her to use a mouth wash. Dry lips would be prevented by a smear of Vaseline™. Clothes and bed linen should be kept fresh. If the child is dressed, she should wear loose, absorbent clothing, such as cotton.

Encourage the child to take a nap during the day. She should not be left on her own for too long, particularly if she is a very young child. Illness in babies can develop very quickly, so you should constantly check them for signs of accelerating illness. The temperature should be checked regularly.

REGRESSIVE BEHAVIOUR

When a child is ill, her behaviour may regress to that of a younger age group. A child who can normally concentrate well may find it impossible to do more than play with toys and equipment that would normally be considered too young. She may start wetting the bed again, having been completely dry for some time. This is absolutely normal and there is no point in trying to stimulate the child with new toys and activities. Simple jigsaws and books outgrown come into their own again.

Try to ignore any bedwetting or any whingeing behaviour. As soon as the child is better she will revert to her usual sunny self.

Infection

Infection is the most common cause of illness in young children and, if frequent, can cause developmental delay and slow down growth. As a nanny, it is important that you know the different types of infection, how they are communicated to others, and how to prevent the spread of infection.

Infection results from invasion of the body by pathogenic (disease causing) organisms.

The main organisms are:
- bacteria such as whooping cough
- viruses such as chickenpox
- fungi such as ringworm
- protozoa such as dysentery.

To grow and multiply, these organisms need moisture, warmth, food and time. Once in the body, they multiply rapidly: this is called the incubation period. Although children are infectious during the incubation period, they begin to display signs and symptoms and feel unwell only at the end of this time.

Infection is spread by:
- droplets: sneezing and coughing
- touch: contact with people or equipment
- eating or drinking infected food and water
- through cuts and grazes on the body.

GOOD PRACTICE IN PREVENTING CROSS-INFECTION

1 Wash hands before handling and eating food.
2 Wash hands after using the lavatory.
3 Keep rooms well ventilated, avoiding overcrowding.
4 Wash and disinfect toys and equipment regularly.
5 Discourage contact with unwell children.
6 Clean the lavatory and bathroom daily.

7   Clean up all spills immediately.
8   Use disposable gloves for First Aid, cleaning up body fluids and changing nappies.
9   Maintain regular trips out of doors.
10 Keep pets clean and healthy.
11 Use paper tissues for wiping noses and disposing of them at once in a covered bin.
12 Select, store and prepare food carefully.
13 Clear the table immediately after meals, not allowing food to be left about.

The quarantine period is the time a person with an infection is capable of transmitting that infection to another person. Hygiene and immunisation play an important part in preventing the spread of infection.

Minor ailments

Most children suffer from mild ill health from time to time. Recognising the signs early on (see below) will prevent the conditions turning into something more serious.

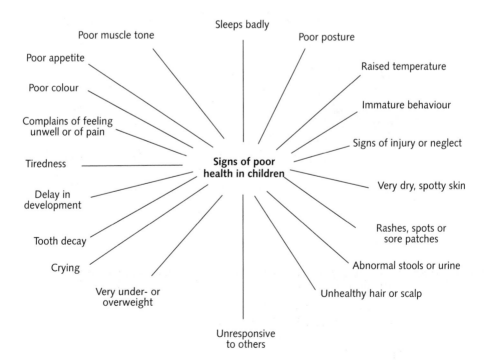

Signs of poor health

UPPER RESPIRATORY TRACT INFECTIONS

The areas of the mouth, nose and throat are the first to be attacked by viruses as they are breathed in. Children are very prone to colds as they are frequently in contact with new organisms and have yet to build up their own immune systems. The main sign of a cold is a runny nose. The discharge is thin at first, becoming thicker after a day or two. The nose can feel blocked, and the child may wish to pick and scratch it. The lining of the nose is more fragile, and will bleed easily. Caring for the child will consist of offering plenty of fluids, checking to see if the child has a fever, teaching the child to use disposable tissues and to blow her own nose, and keeping her warm within a well ventilated room.

A cough can be caused by direct infection of the throat or by nasal mucus dripping from the back of the nose. Coughs cause anxiety but serve a purpose in pushing back infected mucus that threatens the lungs. A cough indicates a more serious illness when it presents with other symptoms such as:

■ difficulty in breathing
■ pallor or blueness
■ thick sticky mucus coming from the lungs
■ traces of blood
■ choking
■ vomiting.

It may be necessary to seek medical advice.

A sore throat may develop on its own, or be accompanied by a cold, and may last only a day or two. It is often present in childhood infections. If a child refuses to drink, has swollen pus-covered tonsils, has a high temperature or is drowsy or dizzy, the situation should be discussed with the parents and the GP consulted.

LOWER RESPIRATORY TRACT INFECTIONS

Infections that spread into the lung tissue are more serious than upper respiratory tract infections. Croup may occur in children between the ages of six months and four years. The child is usually hoarse, with a barking cough, may have some difficulty in breathing, and will appear distressed. A doctor should see all children with croup.

RASHES

Rashes (see page 86) are a sign that the child's body is reacting to an irritation or infection of some type. As long as there are no other symptoms, a rash on its own is rarely a sign of serious illness and usually disappears as quickly as it comes. How a rash looks is generally less important than where it is on the body. There are three main types of rash:

■ rashes all over the body, accompanied by other symptoms, such as a cold and a raised temperature usually indicate a viral infection
■ rashes all over the body, with no signs of ill health will often irritate the child

and are an allergic reaction to something. This needs to be discussed with the parents, for, if the cause is discovered, it can be eliminated. The child may need to be referred to the GP

- rashes appearing on only one part of the body, for example nappy rash and cradle cap. Where it is sited, will often suggest the cause of the rash. If it does not heal within a few days, encourage the parents to seek GP advice.

If there is no obvious cause for a rash, it might be a symptom of stress.

STOMACH ACHES AND PAINS

Stomach aches are a symptom of an upset somewhere in the body, not necessarily the abdomen. Children with tonsillitis, urinary tract infections or middle ear infections may well complain of stomach ache. Stomach aches may have different causes, from mere overeating to more serious conditions such as appendicitis. In most cases there is nothing to worry about, but on rare occasions it is the first sign of a real emergency, so it is best to play safe.

In children, the pain is generally caused by an infection, an inflammation or a change in the activity of the bowel. Many school children complain of stomach ache in response to stress. It may not have a physical cause, but the pain is real, as the disturbed central nervous system that controls the contractions of the stomach and intestines intensifies the contractions. The pain can be so severe the child cannot eat or drink.

You should contact the parents or GP if:

- the child cannot be comforted, and is refusing food and drink
- there is any swelling, or she refuses to let you touch where it hurts
- she is sick, but the pain continues
- she vomits greenish yellow matter
- she has crying spasms, turns pale and vomits
- there are other signs of illness, such as raised temperature or diarrhoea
- she is lethargic
- the pain is mild, but it is mentioned repeatedly over several days.

The child's behaviour is the best guide to the seriousness of the stomach ache. Cuddle and reassure the child. Give her small sips of plain water to drink. Encourage her to rest on a sofa or a bed. She may prefer to lie against a pillow. Have a bowl ready in case she vomits. Warmth may help, so you could offer a well-covered hot water bottle. It is best not to offer anything to eat. If the pain is severe or continues for more than 20 minutes, contact the parents or GP.

VOMITING

Hold the child over a bowl, while supporting the upper body with your free hand. Be reassuring. After the vomiting, wipe the child's face with a sponge or cloth wrung out in tepid water. Encourage her to sip a drink of water slowly to replace fluid loss, and remove the taste from the mouth. Try to get the child to lie quietly on a bed or sofa, keeping the bowl handy. A small baby who vomits can dehydrate quickly, so a doctor should be consulted at once.

Rashes	
Condition	**Description of rash**
Hand, foot and mouth disease	A sparse rash of greyish white, tiny blisters with a red halo. It is seen inside the mouth, on the tongue and on the palms of the hands and the soles of the feet. It lasts 3–5 days and then fades rapidly. Occasionally it spreads to the buttocks.
Cold sores	Sore, painful blisters near the lips and nose that crust after 2–3 days.
Impetigo	Starts as a small blister, generally near the mouth and nose as this part is more vulnerable to infection. Number and size increase, the surface of the skin breaks down, leaving a raw, moist surface that becomes a thick, yellow crust over a reddened, sore area.
Nettle rash	Pale, swollen patches and spots with a red border.
Scabies	Raised, blistery spots and raised, red, discrete spots, generally with scratch marks as it is intensely irritating. Greyish ridges of scabies mite tracks may be seen. Generally between fingers, inside wrists, under the arms, waist and groin.
Eczema	Dry skin, patches of red skin often with small, blistery spots. Inflamed by scratching. Starts on face or skin creases. May become sore or weepy.
Rubella (German measles)	Pale pink spots that start on face and spread to chest and back, perhaps the limbs. On 2nd or 3rd day they become an overall flush. Can last between a few hours and up to 5 days.
Measles	A blotchy rash of dark red spots that spreads from behind the ears to the face, body and limbs over 3–4 days. Up to 2–3 days koplik spots (small white spots) can be seen on the inside of the cheeks at the back of the mouth. Rash fades after 4 days.
Scarlet fever	Small spots of intense red colour that are rough to the touch. It begins with the face and spreads to the neck and chest and then the limbs over 4–5 days. It leaves a pale patch around the mouth.
Chickenpox	3 stages: 1) raised, red, discrete rash of tiny pimples starting on chest and face; 2) spots develop into blisters; 3) after 2–3 days the fluid in the blister becomes cloudy and yellow. It will then form a crust that is intensely irritating. By the third day it will spread to the limbs. In severe cases it can be found on the mucous membrane of the body orifices.
Seborrhoeic eczema	Inflamed, scaly rash behind ears or neck. Associated with cradle cap. Does not irritate.
Heat rash	Small, irritating blisters or pimples on the chest, neck or groin.

EAR INFECTIONS

Ear ache can follow a cold, flu or a throat infection, or develop by itself. The child may have a raised temperature, complain of pain, refuse to drink, and may be seen rubbing or pulling her ear. Seek medical advice as soon as possible. It is likely that an antibiotic will be prescribed, and the child's ears should be examined by the doctor at the end of the course to make sure that the infection has cleared. A child with frequent ear infections may develop a hearing loss.

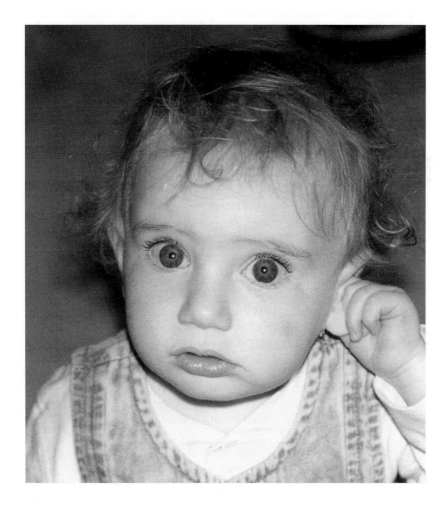

STOOLS AND URINE

As a nanny, you are frequently wiping bottoms and emptying potties. The chart on page 88 will help you to identify any concerns.

Stools and urine	
Condition	**Description of stool**
Normal stool	Soft, clay-like, easy to pass
Underfeeding in a baby	Small, frequent, green stools
Diarrhoea	Frequent, loose watery stools. May contain blood or mucus
Straining	Bright red blood may be seen on the stool
Taking iron medicine	Very dark stools
Bleeding in upper intestine (rare)	Very dark stools
Cystic fibrosis	Large, watery, foul-smelling stools
Constipation	Hard, dry stools, difficult to pass. Hard, dry pellets in a baby
Jaundice	Very pale stool
Inability to digest fats	Large, pale, fatty stool
Threadworms	Worms that look like threads of cotton 1–2 cms. Seen in stool
	Description of urine
Normal urine	Pale, straw-coloured, no smell
Child lacking fluid	Very dark fluid
Jaundice	Very dark fluid
Urinary tract infection	Frequent passing of small amounts. May smell fishy and child may complain of pain
Diabetes	Frequent passing of urine containing sugar

ESCALATION OF MINOR ILLNESSES

Minor illnesses need to be taken seriously and appropriate treatment given to the child. She will need to be observed closely. A neglected troublesome cough can become pneumonia.

A minor illness is becoming serious if the child:

- has a fit
- has a temperature with a stiff neck
- has a temperature with a severe headache
- has a temperature with photophobia (dislike of light)
- has a headache with sickness and dizziness
- is drowsy
- is becoming dehydrated
- becomes quiet or limp
- is in pain
- loses consciousness
- has difficulty breathing

- develops noisy breathing
- begins to turn blue.

You should immediately seek medical attention as a matter of urgency for any child in your care presenting any of these signs and symptoms.

Infestations

Infestations are caused by animal parasites that live on and obtain their food from humans. All children are likely to be affected at some time.

HEAD LICE

Head lice are small insects that live in human hair, close to the scalp where they can bite the skin and feed on the blood. Many children are infested by coming into contact with children who are already carrying head lice, and lice show no preference between clean and unwashed hair. The lice lay eggs, called nits, close to the scalp and cement the eggs firmly to the hair. You may think the child has dandruff, but if you try to dislodge it you will find the nits are firmly fixed. The first indicator of head lice is the child scratching her head and complaining of irritation.

You may seek advice from your local chemist. Many people now are unhappy with the chemical shampoos and treatments. The current method recommended by many schools is to apply a conditioner to the child's head, and use a nit comb to remove the nits and lice. Regular brushing and combing will discourage lice. Everyone in the household, including you and the parents, will need checking.

THREADWORMS

Threadworms are small white worms that live in the bowel. They resemble small pieces of white cotton. They can often be seen in the stools. They come out of the bowel at night to lay their eggs around the anus. This causes severe irritation and the child will scratch herself. If the fingers are then placed in the mouth, the cycle of infection will continue.

Constant sleep disruption will cause the child to become drowsy during the day and lack concentration. The whole family will have to be treated. Your local chemist will advise you. Apply the rules of personal hygiene stringently, encouraging careful hand-washing, disinfect the potty each time the child uses it, and be alert to the signs in other children.

FLEAS

Fleas are small insects that jump from host to host and feed on blood. Fortunately, human fleas are rare in the UK but many children and adults are sensitive to fleas that live on cats and dogs. If bitten by a flea it will leave a red mark that irritates and swells. Animals need to be treated regularly to avoid this problem.

More rarely, children may be infested with ringworm, scabies or ticks, when medical advice has to be sought.

Chronic medical conditions

Many children will have a known medical condition that may affect their physical health, their ability to learn, their relationships and their emotional wellbeing. It is important for you to have some knowledge and understanding of these conditions and how it may affect a particular child. At the initial interview with the parents, it will be helpful for you to find out:
- how the child is affected by the illness
- if there are any significant signs and symptoms you should look for
- what actions you should take if any problems arise while the child is in your care
- precise instructions, possible training and permission to administer any medication or therapy required by the child
- knowledge of any side-effects of medication
- if there are any physical restrictions placed on the child.

If you decide to care for a child with a chronic illness, it is important that you reach this decision only after discussing the following points with the parents:
- the cause (where known) and the effect of the condition
- details of all routine medication and therapy required by the child
- possible side-effects of any medication and therapy
- any possible emergency that may arise, and your ability to manage the situation
- possible hospital appointments and admissions
- how to use any special equipment
- insurance cover.

You would need to assess how much support the parents might demand of you and whether you are willing to take on this responsibility, which will take up much of your time and energy. You should also consider the effect on and the reactions of other children in the family. It might be wise to suggest a probationary period, when you can assess how you are coping.

For any child that you care for with a chronic medical condition you must:
- have full knowledge of the condition and its effect on the child
- liaise closely with the parents
- be very familiar with any treatments and medication.

Administering drugs and/or treatment leaves a nanny vulnerable to allegations of malpractice. It is important that, before carrying out any procedure, you have adequate instruction, written permission from the parents, training and insurance cover.

DIABETES

Diabetes is an endocrine disorder where the pancreas gland fails to produce the insulin that controls the amount of sugar or glucose released into the bloodstream. The high level of blood glucose is too much for the kidneys to cope with, and it is discharged in the urine. Signs of diabetes include:

- excessive thirst
- frequent passing of urine
- loss of weight in children.

Children may complain of headache and abdominal pain, and may vomit. Sugar will be found in blood and urine samples. Most children with diabetes require insulin by injection. Each child will have her own diet plan providing a balanced diet, controlling the intake of carbohydrate. Exercise burns calories, so you may need to offer a sensible snack after any vigorous activity. Normal growth is an indication of good diabetic control.

If you care for a child with diabetes you must:
- make sure the child is wearing a diabetic identity disc
- provide meals promptly
- teach other children in the family about diabetes
- help the child to behave as normally as possible
- be very clear about emergency procedures
- understand hypoglycaemia (a drop in blood sugar which may lead to a seizure or the child becoming comatose). Always have an emergency supply of glucose in the house and a Mars™ bar in your pocket when you take the child out
- understand hyperglycaemia (a rise in blood sugar, which may mean that the child needs insulin).

ASTHMA

This is an increasingly common distressing condition, where the muscle walls of the lungs constrict. Excess mucus is produced that blocks the already narrowed passages. Breathing becomes difficult, the child will wheeze and cough, and may choke. It is often associated with allergic conditions such as eczema and hayfever. It may be triggered by exercise, viral infections, smoke, pollen, fur, house dust mites, yeast, dairy food, anxiety and stress.

It is treated by medication, both preventative and curative. Inhalers and nebulisers are often used to administer the medication. Physiotherapy and a well-balanced diet may also form part of the treatment.

If you are caring for a child with asthma you must:
- know the individual triggers
- be very familiar with the medication used by the child, and know how to keep inhalers and nebulisers clean
- encourage normal activities
- observe for any chest infections
- be fully aware of emergency procedures.

Reducing allergens in the home
It is helpful if you:
- damp dust all surfaces regularly
- put soft toys in freezer for twenty-four hours twice a month, and then wash at 60 degrees centigrade or above to kill the mites
- regularly air the house and keep the house well ventilated
- dry all clothing out of doors when the weather is good
- use bleach to kill any fungus present in the bathroom.

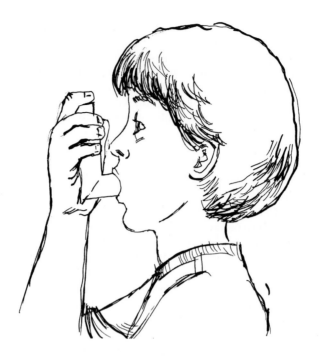

The parents might be encouraged to:

- invest in a high filtration vacuum cleaner
- replace upholstered furniture with leather, wood, plastic or cane
- wash cushions once a month, and never use feather filled ones
- choose short pile carpets or wooden or tiled floors
- avoid carpets in kitchens or bathrooms, where they can become damp
- have heaters and central heating serviced regularly
- take advice about plants and trees in the garden, and having a pet in the house
- avoid compost heaps.

ECZEMA

Children with eczema usually have a very dry skin that becomes inflamed and cracked, making the skin vulnerable to infection. It causes intense irritation and can be very painful. The irritation is made worse when the child is warm, and this can disrupt sleep, leading to tiredness, irritability and lack of concentration. There are times when the skin flares up and is badly affected, and other times when it is completely clear. It can be triggered by infection, irritants such as soap and washing powder, environmental factors, certain foods, exercise, anxiety, medication and handling pets.

If you care for a child with eczema you must:

- know the triggers that cause the allergy
- understand the special attention you may need to give the skin
- keep the child cool when she is showing signs of irritation

- limit messy play if the eczema on the hands is infected. An older child might be willing to wear gloves
- discourage petting strange animals
- teach the other children in the family about the condition, stressing that it is not contagious.

EPILEPSY

There are many different types of epilepsy. Grand mal (tonic/clonic seizure) produces a typical fit, with loss of consciousness, convulsive movements and frothing at the mouth. Petit mal (absences) is less dramatic, and may go unnoticed. The child may look as if she is daydreaming. There is no cure, but modern treatment reduces and prevents frequency of fits.

If you care for a child with epilepsy you must:
- be alert to the signs of an epileptic fit and how to respond
- make sure the child is wearing a medical identity disc
- not leave the child alone for long periods of time
- restrict television viewing, as flickering lights can sometimes result in a fit
- observe the child closely if she is unwell
- teach the other children about epilepsy
- supervise very closely if the child is swimming or cycling.

Ninety per cent of children are healthy most of the time. Nevertheless, it is prudent to be able to recognise illness, however minor, so that steps can be taken to prevent cross-infection, relieve symptoms, prevent complications and ensure that the child receives the care she needs.

7 COMMUNICATION

> **This chapter includes:**
> - Communicating with young children
> - Communicating with adults
> - Managing stress
> - Assertiveness
> - Managing conflict
> - Observation skills and record keeping

Communication allows social and emotional relationships to flourish, is necessary for the transmission of information and ideas and imparts the values and moral codes of society. We show we are attentive to others by the way we listen.

Lack of communication between you and the parents can lead to misunderstandings and this may affect the children in the family. Time needs to be set aside at the beginning and at the end of the day, to discuss any problems that may have occurred, achievements that may have been demonstrated and any changes to the daily routine.

Communication is a two-way process, and efforts will have to be made on both sides. You may be a person with an informal easy manner, and this will be no problem for you. Some people find it harder to find just the right manner.

Communicating with young children

Children learn about the world around them through the senses: touch, sight, hearing, smell and taste. The newborn baby will very quickly recognise the mother by using all her senses. Because of this, the way a stranger handles a baby immediately communicates either a feeling of security or of threat. Someone who wishes to work with young children needs to be responsive, warm and caring, and this will be shown in the way you hold and feed a baby, or bath and dress a toddler.

GOOD PRACTICE WHEN HANDLING YOUNG CHILDREN

1   Approach children calmly and quietly, using your voice to encourage co-operation.
2   Make eye-contact with children before attempting to pick them up.
3   Sit on the floor with younger children; if you tower over them they might feel threatened.

4 Changing a baby's nappy, brushing a child's hair, and helping a child to use the lavatory are all intimate activities and, preferably, should be carried out only when a good relationship has been established. This is one reason why it is so important to have a settling-in period with the parent present, for as long as it takes to establish such a relationship.

5 Children's needs to be cuddled should be met. A child will feel safe and secure if her needs are met swiftly and responsively. Refusing to pick up and cuddle a child who obviously wants you to is not only bad practice, but can be harmful to the development of the child. You also need to respect children who do not wish to be cuddled.

6 Be aware of the child's non-verbal communication.

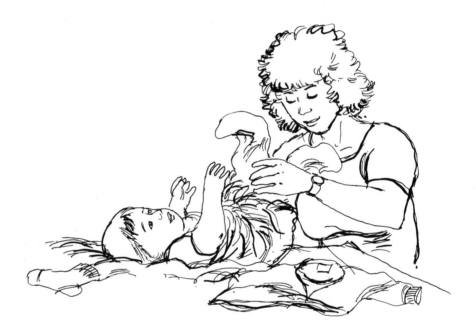

BUILDING A RELATIONSHIP WITH CHILDREN

You are in a unique position when you work as a nanny. The time that you spend in close contact with the children will allow you to have a special and very close relationship with them. You are responsible for their total needs when their parents are not there, in a way you would not be if you were working in a nursery or a school. The children will love and trust you and you need to be aware of the responsibility this brings. This relationship will often continue after you have left the family and, in some cases, for very many years.

You will be an influential role model, contributing to the children's opinions and values. The way that you speak and behave will often be unconsciously copied by the children.

1   Take an interest in each child, not expecting relationships to develop all at once. This takes time.
2   Treat all children equally and fairly.
3   Be positive in how you behave towards and communicate with the children.
4   Give children time to succeed and build on their success.
5   Boost self-esteem and confidence.
6   Give them lots of praise and encouragement.
7   Encourage responsibility and independence.
8   Be calm and patient.
9   Be consistent in the way you manage their behaviour.
10 Treat children with respect, avoiding sarcasm, rudeness and arguments.
11 Be friendly, polite and approachable with children and adults.
12 Avoid expressing concerns about the child in her hearing.

SPEECH

You are obviously aware of the importance of spoken language, and the part it has to play in educational attainment. The sooner that children become fluent in speech and develop their understanding, the better they will get on in school and with their peer group.

From the very first week of life, some people believe even from the womb, babies respond to the voice, learning to recognise the mother's voice and close family voices very quickly. Most language is learnt in the family, and as a nanny you must understand the importance of talking and listening to the children in your care. You should be aware of what a child says, taking care to speak clearly, so as to extend her vocabulary and develop her language skills. Being given time to express herself fully and to be listened to sympathetically, will encourage her language development.

Developing language skills

At about nine months, children gain an understanding of what adults are saying, providing they speak clearly and directly. Soon after this, the first word might appear, and this is the time to start reading books and telling stories. Sitting down quietly with a child and reading a book together should now become a frequent event promoting an interest in books for life. Emphasising important every day words, such as 'drink' and 'bath' will enable her to gain a large vocabulary from an early age.

A recent seven-year study was carried out by Dr Sally Ward, a speech therapist. One group of babies was talked to frequently, emphasising with inflection and gesture the important words in the sentence. A control group, matched for socio-economic status and likely inherited ability, were not treated to the same input. When the children were seven, they were tested for reading ability and IQ. It was found that the first group was significantly in front in both attainment and intelligence. This shows how important it is to converse with babies in a meaningful way, even though you might think they do not understand. This work is described in Dr Ward's book *Baby Talk*, published by Century in March, 2000.

At around two years old, most children will be able to put two words together to make simple sentences. This is the time for quiet, relaxed conversations, always remembering to give the child time to answer. You should never correct or laugh at her grammatical errors, but it will help if you mirror her words, saying it correctly. For example, a child might say 'Daddy buyed me doll', and you could reply, 'It was Daddy who bought it for you, was it?' These mistakes are made because the rules of grammar are being applied, and too much correction might inhibit speech.

Try not to ask children 'closed' questions, when the answer is already known (for example,'What colour are your shoes?'). They will probably think it strange that you do not know your colours! Questions, which require only one-word answers, such as 'Yes' or 'No', do not allow children to extend their vocabulary. If they ask a question to which you do not know the answer, be honest enough to say so, and to discuss ways of discovering the answer together. Asking 'open-ended' questions, such as 'Why do you think some animals have fur?', will help her to develop language skills more quickly.

If you ask a child to carry out a task, it must be explained simply and clearly. Asking children if they would like to help clear up might justify the answer 'No'. They are not necessarily being defiant, but will respond much better if told politely to do it. Never ask them to do several things at once.

Make sure the children are given time to work out what they want to say. Do not anticipate children's speech, let them find their own words. Four-year-olds are very excited by new words, and particularly by those to which they get a reaction. If a child swears, remember this is a normal stage, and the best way to stop the habit is to ignore it. Children do not invent these words, so be aware that careless speech from adults is often copied.

EXTENDING OPPORTUNITIES

You might read a favourite story to a child, recording your voice on a cassette. She will enjoy turning the pages of the book and matching the pictures to the story she can hear on the tape. This helps develop listening skills and manipulation skills while encouraging early reading. You could make a simple puppet of the main character in a story that she enjoys. This will encourage her to look at the book on her own or with a friend, using the puppet to stimulate her imagination.

Some domestic activities, such as cooking and washing up together, usually generate discussion and lively conversation, which will help to extend vocabulary and mathematical and scientific terms. Shopping together will present opportunities for recognising familiar foods, and becoming aware that the symbols on the cans and packages represent the names of the foods. All outings introduce children to the wider environment, and stimulate language and the acquisition of vocabulary.

Julie looks after Simon, who is two years old and Jeannette who is nearly four years. This is Julie's first job and she is enjoying it immensely. The only problem is when Granny visits twice a week and insists on going shopping with her and the children as she has a car.

Instead of allowing the children time to look at all the goodies in the supermarket, Granny always seems to be in a terrific hurry, and looks on shopping as a chore to get through as quickly as possible, rather than as an opportunity to extend the children's language. She also finds it difficult to give the children time to speak, finishing their sentences for them, and correcting their grammar.

1   Why is this a problem for Julie?
2   Should she discuss it with Granny?
3   Should she speak to the parents?

Communicating with adults

A professional nanny needs to develop skills in listening and speech, in writing, and to be aware of her body language.

Listening skills

When communicating, it is as important to develop your listening skills as your speech. Being a 'good' listener does not come naturally to everyone. You need to listen carefully to others, concentrate, look interested and not interrupt, never finishing sentences for the speaker.

Remember that in some circumstances you may not be listening effectively. If you are worried or upset about something, your concentration may be diverted. Other noises or movements in the room may distract you. Your feelings about the person may distort what you hear.

Listening is a positive activity and therefore the good listener does not relax when listening but has to monitor and analyse what is being said in order to make an appropriate response. It may be necessary to indicate to the speaker that you are listening attentively by the use of words such as 'Uhuh' and 'Mmm', which display interest and understanding. Sometimes summarising what the speaker has just said is helpful as it makes you listen carefully, lets the speaker know if the message was communicated correctly, and eliminates misunderstanding which might lead to conflict.

SPOKEN COMMUNICATION

You will be using speech in day-to-day conversations with the children, your employers, other parents and, perhaps, other nannies. There is no better way of communicating than talking with people. Always speak clearly, slowly and expressively, particularly when in formal situations, or when the information you have to convey is particularly important.

Be aware of your listener's background, knowledge and feelings and what your ideas will mean to her or him. If you are speaking on the telephone on behalf of the parents, speak very clearly, a little more slowly than usual and do not allow your voice to drop in tone at the end of the sentence, as this will distort the clarity of your speech. When answering the telephone, give your name and explain who you are. If the call is not for you, write down the message and repeat it to the caller to ensure accuracy. It is sensible to note the telephone number of the caller. See that the message is passed on to your employer as quickly as possible. Personal calls should not be made on the family phone without permission, unless there is an emergency.

Many nannies nowadays are given mobile phones by their employers so that they can be reached at any time, and have no difficulty in reporting any emergency even if they are out of the house. Nannies living in rural areas, who may often be asked to take the children in the car will feel more secure if they can reach help if necessary. It obviously is not safe to continue to drive while using a mobile phone, as research has shown it lowers the driver's concentration and causes accidents.

Activity
List the advantages and disadvantages of being given a mobile phone by your employer.

Some people communicate better with speech than in writing but it may be the other way round. You will need both skills to be an effective nanny.

WRITING SKILLS

A professional person is presumed to be proficient in communicating information, ideas, directions and requests in writing and this will take many different forms. When writing for your own information such as a personal diary or a list of things to remember, you can record this information in whatever way is useful to you.

You may have to write items that need to be shared with the children's parents, such as:
■ observations of the children
■ a diary to share with the family
■ taking and recording telephone messages.
   Whatever you are writing, remember to:
■ be clear about the purpose of your correspondence
■ use short sentences that convey your exact meaning
■ be as neat and legible as possible, checking the spelling and grammar (you may find using a word processor helpful)
■ keep a copy (use a black pen as this will photocopy well)

- date all correspondence
- be professional, sticking to the facts and being objective
- respect confidentiality.

BODY LANGUAGE

Your body is sending out messages at the same time as you are talking and listening. To be effective, all messages should be the same, but sometimes communication is spoilt when body language differs from what is being said.

Think about:

- posture
- eye contact
- facial expression
- energy level
- position of your feet and legs when sitting
- personal space
- touching others.

For example, while engaged in conversation with your employer, positive body language would be maintaining eye contact, smiling, and leaning towards her, while speaking at a moderate rate and in an assuring tone. Negative body language would be yawning, looking or turning away, going off into a daydream and missing cues.

COMMUNICATING WITH OTHER PROFESSIONALS

During your working life as a nanny, you may find yourself in occasional contact with other people from the educational, health and caring professions. A health visitor may visit you if you are working with young babies. You may be asked by the parents to take the children to the infant welfare clinic or health centre for developmental assessments or for immunisations. If the child needs specialist help, such as speech therapy or dental treatment you may be asked to accompany her in place of the parent. You may be involved with staff at pre-school or school. To aid communication you need to be aware of the roles and functions of these professional colleagues.

Activities

1 How would you communicate with parents your concerns about their child's behaviour?
2 How do you encourage parents to share their concerns about their child with you?
3 What communication difficulties have you had in the past with parents? How did you cope with these situations?

Managing stress

Nannies sometimes find themselves in stressful situations. You need to recognise, understand and respond to the causes of stress so as to avoid harming your health or your ability to work in a positive way with children and their families.

CAUSES OF STRESS

Working in a close relationship with parents who may themselves be experiencing stress can generate anxiety. There are life events that can generate a great deal of stress such as divorce, separation, bereavement, unemployment and moving house. In your professional role, stress might, among other factors, result from:

■ taking on too heavy a work load
■ not earning as much as you need
■ not being paid on time
■ not getting enough to eat, or being served food you do not like
■ losing your time off, or having it altered at short notice
■ lack of privacy
■ caring for a child with disruptive and aggressive behaviour
■ dissatisfaction with your job
■ feeling isolated
■ spending too much time on work activities
■ sickness
■ difficult relationships with parents

- taking on responsibilities which are not necessarily part of your job, but which you find difficult to refuse
- parents who fail to keep to the contract of employment.

SIGNS OF STRESS

Signs of stress may include:
- variation in appetite
- insomnia
- tiredness or lethargy
- tearfulness
- tension headaches
- constipation or diarrhoea
- high blood pressure
- lack of concentration
- inability to decide priorities
- lack of interest in life
- feelings of inadequacy
- difficulty in making decisions
- feeling neglected, overworked, tense and anxious
- unable to suppress anger
- low libido.

Employment patterns are changing and many people are expected to contribute more and more in the workplace while job security is decreasing. This may have a knock-on effect on you, if parents frequently do not arrive home at the expected time. If one of the parents becomes unemployed or redundant your services may no longer be required. Someone who is stressed may find themselves often ill, and having to take time off work. As so many people rely on your good health, your stress would affect many other people.

CASE STUDY

Carole lives in with the McKenzie family. The parents run their own business that is going through a period of rapid growth and expansion. This means that they are often late home, phoning at the last minute to warn Carole that they will not be in for dinner and expecting her to care for the children until they get home, not a normal part of Carole's job. They have asked her to work several weekends when she should be enjoying her free time.

The children are always asking for their parents and the oldest child is becoming withdrawn while the toddler is being very disruptive and aggressive. The baby takes longer to go to sleep, being used to her mother settling her down. Carole is also missing the adult conversation she is used to in the evenings.

1 Should Carole discuss the situation with the parents? How might she approach this?
2 Is there anything she can do to alleviate her own stress?
3 How might she help the children?

COPING WITH STRESS

First you have to admit and recognise that you are suffering from stress and discover how you got yourself into this situation. If it is the job itself that is the main cause, it may be difficult to extricate yourself because you have responsibilities and financial commitments. You must face up to the situation, be honest with yourself, look at alternative strategies such as working part-time, or even changing families. If you cannot change the situation, look for further help. Think about the following:

- discussion with the parents to review your job description and contract
- an appointment with your GP to discuss any symptoms you may have and to find out what sources of help are available
- personal counselling to help you reflect on your lifestyle and make possible changes
- courses on assertiveness, time management and relaxation techniques.

Coping strategies
- Learn to say no.
- Learn how to express your opinions and feelings.
- Look for support from and offer support to other nannies.
- Try to relax on your days off and on holidays.
- Manage your time more effectively, plan your day in advance.
- Look after yourself by eating a healthy diet with plenty of fruit and vegetables, limiting fats and sugars.
- Take regular exercise.
- Do not rely on nicotine, alcohol, or caffeine.
- Relax in a hot bath after work.
- Apply heat to the body using a heat pad or a hot water bottle. This may reduce muscular tension.
- Try massage, using aromatic oils.
- Explore techniques such as yoga or meditation to reduce the effects of stress. They may also boost your ability to avoid becoming stressed.
- Develop new interests and hobbies.
- Talk about your feelings to others and recognise your achievements.
- Be prepared to be flexible and do not live by rigid rules.
- Remember the good positive things that have happened and do not focus on failures or difficulties.

Assertiveness

In response to any problem, people tend to react in one of four ways:
- aggressively, hurting and upsetting others, perhaps making them feel inferior
- indirectly aggressively, manipulating or humiliating someone, arousing feelings of guilt
- passively, avoiding conflict and refusing to make choices, allowing other people to take advantage of them

- assertively, with a confident approach, presenting their own opinions while not belittling the other person.

Each will have a different effect on other people and we will feel differently about ourselves and the way we have behaved.

It is particularly important for a professional person to be assertive, especially a nanny who has so many demands on her time. Learning to be assertive allows you to be open in expressing your feelings and needs, and encourages you to stand up for your rights and respect the rights of others. It has nothing to do with aggression, but is a technique that allows you to relate to others in an open and honest way, discussing problems and not personalities. Your assertive behaviour should encourage others to be assertive.

Being assertive will enable you to:
- handle conflict, dealing with difficult situations where people are angry or upset
- be more confident, decisive and comfortable in your role
- communicate better, feeling able to express your views, identify problems and work together with others in finding solutions
- reduce levels of stress
- develop professionally and personally.

Once you are clear about your expectations, they become easier to state and therefore to achieve. Once you start to assert yourself, the approach is simple. You state your needs, rights and opinions in a clear way that is easily understood.

CASE STUDY

Jenny has decided to care for children on a part-time basis, so she will have enough time for a course of further study. The mother of the children has been admitted to hospital for emergency surgery and is expected to take some time to recover. The father has been pressurising Jenny to look after the children full-time for an unspecified period.

1   How should Jenny respond?
2   How might she help the family, while meeting her own needs?

Managing conflict

If there are conflicts between you and one or both of the parents, the children you care for will sense the atmosphere and may become distressed. For example, if the parents suddenly went away with the children on holiday, they might expect you to take your holiday at the same time, even though you had already booked a fortnight in Majorca with your boyfriend at a later date. Another example would be if one of the parents wanted you to smack the children when they misbehaved and you rightly felt that this would be wrong. Whatever the reason, the only way to resolve a conflict is to communicate, and find out exactly what the problem is.

If a conflict exists, do not ignore it and hope that it will disappear on its own. Address the issue promptly but not impulsively, allowing yourself and the parent time to express views objectively, and find a solution that suits both of you. You may both have to make compromises and show some flexibility. It is often useful to arrange a later date to look again at the problem, and see if your solution is working. Some tension within a relationship may be beneficial. In working together to sort out disagreements, people may begin to understand themselves and others better, the decisions made are likely to be thought through more and the process may be stimulating. If conflict exists, ignoring it and refusing to discuss it can be harmful and totally disrupt your work practice. A knowledge of assertiveness skills will help you put your view clearly and purposefully.

Sometimes, due to a personality clash, or inflexible rigid ideas, it is impossible to come to an agreement and for the sake of the children you may decide to seek other employment. This rarely happens, if enough time and effort have been put into the original interview and the drawing up of the contract.

As you become more experienced, you will become more aware of your communication skills. If you feel that you need a little help, this is readily available, as your local college will run courses in all areas of communication.

Observation skills and record keeping

You are observing and assessing children in your care all the time, and are likely to have the advantage of working closely with the children you care for over a long period. In this way, you get to know them very well, but it is still of value to you and to the children to sometimes step back and watch in an objective way what the children are doing and how they are behaving. Observing children in this manner, and recording what you observe, is an integral part of the role of any professional person who works with children.

THE VALUE OF OBSERVATIONS

Observations are valuable because they help you to:
- understand the basic needs of children: for love, food, shelter and stimulation
- become sensitive and perceptive in meeting these needs, and sometimes in assisting the parents in doing so. By recording objective observations, you learn in a practical way to become aware of these needs, and how to meet them
- share information with parents. For example, your observation of a child who is often tired, and reluctant to take part in any energetic activity, might lead you to discuss this with the child's parents. At another time, you might care for a child who does not like her hair being washed. Being aware of this might prompt you to discuss it with the parents, and find out the reason for her fears
- encourage the child's social development. Observing the way that the children play with friends, it is easy to see if they may need help in relating to

others. Some children are more skilled at relating to adults, while others appear shy with strangers

■ identify and understand changes in children's behaviour. Careful observations are useful in this case, as the change in behaviour might have a physical cause, such as the onset of illness, or it might be an emotional response to family problems or changes. You will grow to understand that all children are individuals and will behave and react differently in similar situations. For example, visiting a farm will be an enjoyable experience for most children, but the child you care for might cling to you, and appear nervous in the presence of large animals

■ understand what might provoke a child to behave in a particular fashion. For example, a child who is particularly fractious just before mealtimes, may not be eating enough at each meal and perhaps need smaller more frequent meals

■ understand normal development, so that if the pace of development of a child in your care is outside the normal range, either advanced or delayed, you can discuss this with the parents

■ be aware of the possible hazards in the home. Linking this with your awareness of developmental stages will allow you to protect the children from danger

■ be alert to signs of ill health. This could be obvious, such as a sudden skin rash, or a child who vomits, or lethargy in a child who is usually active and full of beans. It may be less obvious during the incubation period of an infectious disease, but a noted change in behaviour might cause you concern

■ plan activities for the children that are age-appropriate and will extend and promote learning and development.

You know a great deal about the children you care for. This knowledge needs to be objective, not based on assumptions and value judgements. Being able to observe in an unbiased manner is not instinctive. If several people see a person being mugged, you would probably get many different versions of the incident, and many descriptions of the perpetrator. People's perceptions are coloured by their past experiences, expectations, desire to please, fears and anxieties and even last night's television viewing.

Having preconceived ideas about the character or competence of individual children may influence your assessment. You need to be honest when observing children, and not add anything that makes the observation easier to understand or more interesting. It is important to share information with the parents so make sure your observations are tactful and sensitive.

The children you care for may have been brought up differently from the way you have. In their family, there may be different expectations of children's behaviour. For example, some children may have been expected to take on some domestic tasks at an early age, while in other families the boys are waited on. Some families may discourage their children from messy play, or dressing up in clothes of the opposite gender. The greater the understanding and knowledge you have of other cultures and various child-rearing practices, the less likely you are to make value judgements based on your own upbringing and background, and the more likely you are to view them as individuals.

Melanie, an experienced nanny, was worried about Daniel, aged two and half years, who was aggressive and disruptive. He was the work of three children! She seemed to be constantly saying, 'Stop it, Daniel!' She spoke to his mother about his behaviour and was assured that he was an angel at the weekends when Melanie had her free time. She decided to make a daily record of Daniel's behaviour to show Daniel's mother in a professional way how he behaved when Melanie was caring for him.

After keeping this record for a week, it became obvious that many of the fights were not his fault. Matthew, his older brother, was found to be teasing him and calling him names. When Matthew started school the following month, Daniel's behaviour improved beyond measure.

1   Why was keeping this record good professional practice?
2   Why might Matthew be behaving in this way?
3   Why do you think Matthew did not tease Daniel at the weekends?

EVALUATION AND ASSESSMENT

Some observations may reveal to you that a course of action or a medical referral is needed. Some actions you may be able to carry out on your own. For example, if you discover that a four-year-old about to start school, is unable to use scissors in a practical way, you will be able to encourage her in learning this skill, and give her plenty of practice. On the other hand, if you suspect that a child may have a hearing loss, it is important that you bring this to the parents' attention with the facts that you have collected from your observations, and encourage them to seek medical advice as quickly as possible.

8 OPPORTUNITIES FOR PLAY AND LEARNING

> **This chapter includes:**
> ■ **Play**
> ■ **Planning and preparing activities**
> ■ **Outings**

The amount of time the child spends with you makes your role in encouraging play and learning crucial. It is recognised that children learn very rapidly in the first few years of life and you will need to provide stimulating play opportunities that will encourage their curiosity and imagination.

Play

We all like to play. Adults play games, exercise, dance, explore creative activities, go on holiday, visit museums and art galleries, and indulge in passive activities, such as watching television, going to the cinema and theatre, listening to music and reading. All these activities adults find stimulating and enhance their enjoyment of life.

Children need the same opportunities, and you will be experienced in offering play activities to the children in your care. For them, stimulating play is vital as it is mainly by play that children learn.

For children, passive play such as watching videos, is not as valuable as active play in which they participate. That is not to say that there is no place for television, but the child learns more if she watches with an adult, who helps to interpret what is happening. Some parents may indicate how much television they wish their children to view and you will, of course, respect this. On the other hand, television programmes may be part of the routine. When used wisely, television is a useful educational tool.

Be very selective in the programmes you allow the children to watch. It is a good idea to record some programmes, such as 'Sesame Street' or 'Blue Peter', and have them available to show the children at a time that suits you. The children will gain more from watching if you are with them to answer questions and help them participate.

Children's play reflects intellectual ability and development and has been called 'children's work'. It is an integral part of the daily life and the promotion of all-round development. Through play, the child experiences life and learns to understand the world and her place in it. Play can be social, when children interact with each other; some researchers looking on play as a process of socialisation.

The baby plays from birth, the first 'toy' being the mother's breast. From this stage, play develops through several stages: solitary, parallel (playing alongside another child or adult), associative play with other children leading to co-operative play, involving planning and games with complicated rules.

There are many different types of play, indoor and out, structured and spontaneous. The diagram on page 112 describes these.

Nannies should avoid intervening too frequently and attempting to impose too rigid a structure on children's play. By interaction with the children, you can enrich the play, as long as this is done sensitively.

Planning and preparing activities

However familiar you are with providing play opportunities for children, you will need to remember that all activities should promote the children's all-round development.

Through your knowledge of the children and of the norms of development, you will be able to plan your activities with the children's needs in mind. This will help you to be aware of what is happening and when you need to step in to move the play forward. There will be many occasions when you feel that unstructured and spontaneous activities will be fun for all concerned, and allow children to use

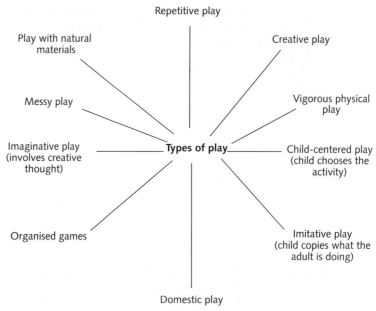

Types of play

their imagination. There are very few activities that do not have some value. The important point is that you are aware of the value of the activities you are planning and preparing.

Play and activities should start from birth. It is not always possible to provide an activity in which all the children in the family can participate. You might have to wait until the younger children are resting before offering a more complex activity to the older children.

Let older children help you with routine domestic activities. Laying the table, preparing food, sorting the clean washing, and putting away the shopping all require mathematical skills, concentration, and a good vocabulary and is part of their social development. Growing independence gives children self-esteem and confidence, all of which aid learning in other areas.

MESSY PLAY

Some activities provided for children are not adult directed. You will just need to provide the materials and observe how they use it, without expecting any end product. Your employer will have to be very tolerant of mess if you allow messy play to take place inside the home, but it is possible to do most of the activities outside on a fine day.

Messy play, such as playing with cooked spaghetti mixed with liquid detergent and colouring, or making hand and feet prints with thick paint, is enjoyable for all children, but particularly so for the youngest ones. A large sheet of paper can be attached to a fence in the garden, and paint in squeezy bottles can be squirted at it. Finger painting comes into this category; paints and paste are mixed together, and patterns made in the mixture with the fingers. Older children might like to print their creations.

NATURAL MATERIALS

Water
Water is an indestructible material and children can bang and splash without harm. Playing with water, which is a natural activity that takes place every day in the bath, allows many mathematical and scientific concepts to be explored. Some children will enjoy playing with the bath toys and finding out about floating and sinking, while others might enjoy playing with water on its own, finding it a soothing and relaxing experience. Children learn that water comes in many forms: as snow, rain, steam, and ice, and is essential for life.

Sand
You would not provide sand indoors in the house but if your family has a sand pit in the garden, playing with sand is an enjoyable and educational experience. Dry sand is relaxing and therapeutic to play with. A great deal can be learnt with the use of various tools. It is not suitable for very young children, unless closely supervised, as they tend to throw it around and get it in their eyes and hair as well as eat it. Wet sand is suitable for all age groups. It can be used as a modelling

material, and can be combined with blocks and cars and other small toys to stimulate the imagination.

Mud

Once children are mobile, most of them find out about mud quite quickly, and should be allowed to play with it outside if they are fully immunised. You will need to check that the garden is free from pesticides. You should check with the parents to make sure children are protected against tetanus. It is one of the most enjoyable of natural materials for young children; it costs nothing and is readily available in every garden. Mud can be mixed with water to give enjoyable sensory experiences, and can be seen to dry out to revert to dry soil. Small animals found in the mud give interest and pleasure to children, who often need to be persuaded to return them to their natural habitat.

Whenever children are exploring natural materials, particularly mud, they should wear their oldest clothes. You can throw these into the washing machine when they have finished playing, so parents will not be worried that delicate or special clothes are getting spoilt.

MODELLING MATERIALS

Plasticine™, dough and clay are all used for modelling. It is unlikely that you will use clay in the house, even outside, as it is extremely messy and needs close supervision.

Plasticine™

This useful manufactured material is good for developing manipulative skills, and for making models with older children. It is much cleaner and less messy than other malleable materials. It can get hard very easily and needs storing in a warm environment.

Dough

Dough can be made in many ways and presented to children in a range of colours, and the children will enjoy participating in the mixing. By adding other ingredients, apart from the essential flour and water, different kinds of elasticity can be achieved. Salt should always be added as a preservative, and it will also ensure that children do not eat it. Dough should appear attractive, have enough elasticity without sticking to surfaces or fingers, and should last for at least a week in a sealed plastic container, kept in a refrigerator

Activity

Experiment with different dough recipes using various flours, ingredients and colours. Make a note of the recipe you find most successful.

You might like to involve older children in making dough with you.

COOKING

From a very young age, children enjoy watching and helping adults prepare and cook food. Children learn about food hygiene and balanced meals, how to make choices in the supermarkets for taste and value, and where different foods come from. It is possible today to buy food from all around the world, and by using recipes from various countries children learn about a range of cultures in a most enjoyable way.

'Cooking' covers a wide range of activities, from making a sandwich to producing a complicated meal. It is important that the children do as much as possible for themselves, being involved from the preparation stage through to eating the food. By helping to plan some of their meals, older children gain shopping skills, such as making lists, choosing ingredients and handling money.

IMAGINARY PLAY

Imaginary play grows out of imitative play. Babies from a very early age imitate adults in games of Peek-a-boo, waving goodbye and copying actions. Later, children do not need a direct role model in front of them, but will start to use their memory, pouring out imaginary cups of tea for all and sundry, and pretending to eat non-existent food.

At around two years, children start to take on roles. One will be the 'mummy', and another the 'daddy', and this will gradually extend to include the baby, the big sister, the nanny, and even a visiting aunt. As children become older, role play will be extended to other people familiar in their lives or from books, such as the nurse, and the firefighter. Providing dressing-up clothes often stimulates the imagination of the children. You might ask the parents to give you some clothes they no longer wear that can be altered for the children to use. Hats, scarves, belts, handbags and shoes will all add to the play. Dresses that are pretty and sparkly will be in great demand. There is a wide variety of dressing-up clothes that can be bought, from tutus to astronauts' outfits.

For some children, acting out a role can be a release of emotions through pretending to be someone else. A child waiting to go into hospital will find it very useful to be a make-believe patient, as a way of expressing emotions and fears. Some children, who may be withdrawn or shy, may still have difficulty in expressing their emotions. Puppets or a toy telephone can be a great help here, as the child uses them to voice hidden feelings. Ready-made puppets should be introduced cautiously, as small children can be fearful of a toy that seems to have a life of its own.

As children are small, vulnerable people, they enjoy acting out roles of super-heroes. It makes them feel empowered and strong, and is a boost to their self-esteem. There can be a negative side as some super-heroes on the television appear to children to be invincible and under-fives cannot always tell fact from fiction. Some research seems to show that violence shown on television does not necessarily lead to violent behaviour, but it certainly has some effect on some children. This is another reason not to use the television as a babysitter, and shows how necessary it is for you to sit with the children, helping them learn and discriminate between fact and fantasy.

Children play with dolls in different ways at each stage of their development. Once babies start to walk, they will use the doll as any other inanimate object, just holding onto it anywhere (usually the feet) and dragging it after them. At about two years, some children will start to cuddle the doll, treating it more as a baby, particularly if there has been a recent birth in the family. This doll might come in for some very hard knocks! A little later on, children enjoy bathing dolls, dressing (but mainly undressing) them and taking them out for walks in a pushchair. At about six years, children might play with several dolls, having pretend tea parties or schoolrooms. Many girls start to collect dolls, such as Barbie™, and there is often rivalry in the collecting of their clothes and artefacts. Some boys might have dolls, such as Action Man™, but rarely collect them in the same way.

Small-scale models of people, animals, vehicles, dolls' houses, and items of domestic equipment are often used in imaginary play. They are familiar to the children, and the play allows them to relax, extend and develop their language.

Activity
List ten toys you think encourage creativity in children.

PAINTING AND DRAWING

All children should be offered frequent opportunities to paint and draw when they feel inclined. When very young, before fluent speech has developed, spontaneous drawing and painting is a most valuable means of expression. This is very much reduced if adults insist on questioning children about their paintings, and suggest additions to the work. Smaller homes might find it difficult to accommodate a painting easel but, if there is the space, it will encourage children to paint in a creative and free way.

Painting, in particular, often allows children to express emotions that they find difficult to put into words. Painting and drawing encourage imagination and creativity, and lend themselves to pattern creation.

A supply of paper, washable markers, crayons and chalks encourage children to draw. This activity is more manageable than painting, and much easier to clear up!

BRICKS, BLOCKS AND CONSTRUCTION SETS

A bag of bricks is the most versatile piece of equipment that any child can have access to from the age of one year onwards. Blocks can be hard and made out of wood or plastic, they can be soft and manufactured from rubber, cotton or foam, and they can be brightly coloured or in natural wood – but they are all construction toys and are there to build with.

At first, children will play on their own, building a tower of bricks, and enjoying knocking it down again. This leads on to four-year-olds planning small and large constructions together, playing co-operatively and imaginatively.

PUZZLES AND SIMPLE GAMES

Jigsaw puzzles are familiar to all young children. Jigsaws range from very simple inset boards for the youngest children, to very intricate puzzles for adults. Sometimes children will choose easy puzzles when they are feeling the need for reassurance, while at other times they will enjoy the challenge of more demanding jigsaws. It is important that no pieces are missing, particularly for the younger children, as this spoils the pleasure of completing a task satisfactorily.

Board games similarly come in varying degrees of difficulty. Most are not suitable for the under-fours as the children will not have yet gained the concept of taking turns, and may get upset at having to wait, and spoil the game for their older siblings. Most games are a variation of Ludo or Snakes and Ladders.

Matching games, such as Picture Lotto and Connect™, help children to see similarities and differences, and to match like with like. This is a pre-reading skill and can be played by one child alone, or with a group of friends.

Card games, such as Snap, Go Fish, Pairs or Sevens, are enjoyed by children of four years upwards. Snap or Pairs cards can be made quite easily by you and the children, using pictures or familiar photographs

ACTIVITIES THAT AID MANIPULATIVE SKILLS

Children enjoy threading beads and cotton reels, and again these are graded in order of difficulty, the younger children finding the larger beads the easiest. Pegboards and mosaic pieces help children to make patterns. Sewing cards help children to be more skilful with their fingers as they are asked to go in and out of holes with a lace or a threaded needle. This may lead to an interest in embroidery or tapestry at a later date, and can also be used to make presents for people in the family.

BOOKS AND STORIES

Enjoyment of books and stories usually starts in the home. Before a child is a year old, she enjoys looking at pictures or photographs while being cuddled by an adult. Nurturing this love of books is probably the key factor in the later acquisition of reading skills. Young children in particular, derive great pleasure in being told stories. These can be personalised, either being tales from the story-teller's past, or stories where the listener becomes the centre of the tale. Being told or read a story is delightful and relaxing. Most children enjoy being read to before settling down to sleep. This may be something that your employer wishes to do herself, although a recent survey has shown that only 23 per cent of children have a story read to them at bedtime.

Poetry for older children will enrich their vocabulary and let them know that it is acceptable to express emotions. For younger children humorous verse is a good introduction. For all children, it can, like books, open up a world of fantasy and imagination.

COMPUTER GAMES

Many children from a very young age enjoy computer games. They can be educational and need not be isolating if two or more children play with them. As with television viewing, computer game playing needs to be supervised and monitored. Apart from widening their knowledge, they also enhance their manipulative skills. Many CD ROMs are linked with the National Curriculum. Young children should not be allowed to touch the back of the equipment or linking cables. The monitor should be at an angle that makes children look up slightly when they are using it, as otherwise it might affect their posture.

PLAYING OUTSIDE

Nearly every activity that takes place in the house can equally well be taken into the garden if the weather permits. A safe fenced garden is a bonus for young children, to exercise and let off steam, to practice their developing physical skills and to build self-confidence. Fresh air and exercise promotes good health. A garden allows children freedom to investigate and explore their environment with little adult restriction.

The garden provides a stimulus for all the senses and an opportunity for a range of imaginary play experiences. Children must be dressed according to the weather, protected against the sun as well as the rain.

Activity
If you do not have access to a garden, how would you ensure that the children get enough fresh air and exercise?

Outings

There will be times when you will be taking the children out to go shopping, visiting the local park or beach or the railway or fire station, or visiting a friend for tea. Perhaps you might be taking the children to places of entertainment, such as the zoo, a farm or a theme park, paying a visit to child-centred museums or art galleries, children's concerts and theatres, the cinema, and play and leisure centres.

Any type of outing is valuable in widening and enriching children's experience of the outside world. As a general rule, outings should be short and simple for the younger child. Very young children do not enjoy long journeys and some of the more exciting places to visit may leave them unimpressed. They will find an impromptu picnic on the beach or a leisurely walk around the park at their own pace just as enjoyable as a trip to a theme park. What is of most value to the young child is the undivided attention and interest of an adult.

With very young children, it is wise to avoid places where:

■ there are very large open spaces and a child might wander off
■ there is a lot of traffic and pollution
■ animal droppings are not cleared up promptly
■ there is a great deal of litter dropped, such as in some markets
■ the children have to be quiet and keep still for a long time
■ it is difficult to supervise more than one child safely, such as in a playground with swings, high obstacle courses and slides, and unsupervised water play or
■ sandpits are not covered at night to prevent animals from fouling them
■ only junk food is available.

Some children need to be held by the hand at all times near a road; some should not be allowed to climb too high; some just need watching like a hawk at all times!

All outings, even the simplest, need to be well planned and prepared. You would not dream of taking a baby anywhere without a change of nappy, wet wipes, a bottle or drink and even a change of clothes. In the summer, adequate protection in clothing and sun block needs to be put in the bag, and in winter-time additional warm clothing and cream to prevent chafing if it becomes very cold and windy. It is a good idea to carry a small emergency First Aid kit, containing anti-histamine cream, medicated wipes and plasters. Older children may want to take games equipment, bikes, and dolls. Comfort objects should not be forgotten, especially if the outing is long and the child is likely to become tired at the end of the day.

It is never too early to start teaching children basic rules of safety, and making sure that they know their address and home telephone number. When in parks and on beaches, always identify a highly visible point, such as a café, where children should go if they should become temporarily separated and reinforce road safety at every opportunity.

SPECIAL CLASSES AND ACTIVITIES

Some homes are not suitable for messy activities and not all homes have gardens. Depending on where you live, there are many special activities provided by outside agencies. You might like to find out what is available locally to you if you have not already done so. Popular activities for children include swimming, gymnastics, dance classes, horse riding, creative art classes, martial arts and self-defence, and football.

You might find other ideas advertised in your local paper and in special issues of magazines that occasionally publish classes and activities for very young children. These classes entertain and promote skills and the children will meet other children of a similar age. You may also make friends with other nannies in your neighbourhood.

Taking pleasure in watching the children learning from the activities you have provided will be a rewarding part of your job.

9 MANAGING CHILDREN'S BEHAVIOUR

> **This chapter includes:**
> ■ Factors that influence behaviour
> ■ Common causes of challenging behaviour
> ■ Managing unwanted behaviour
> ■ Issues that cause conflict
> ■ The smacking debate

Behaviour is the way in which a person conducts herself in relation to other people. It is the response to an action. Parents will wish their children to behave in a sociably acceptable way, and may have clear guidelines on how this can be achieved. In your training you will have understood why children behave in certain ways and that you need to be consistent in the way you manage children's behaviour. This is an area where agreement with the parents should have been reached during the interview, but there still may be some behaviour that may cause conflict.

Behaviour is learnt through the child observing the people closest to her and the way they react to her, both verbally and non-verbally. Rewards and punishments shape behaviour. The reward may just be praise and encouragement, and the punishment a disapproving look, but it will have an effect.

Knowledge of the normal development of children will help you to understand what behaviour is appropriate at what age and stage of development. For example, a toddler is not expected to be completely toilet trained, but regularly wetting and soiling pants would be worrying behaviour in a five-year-old.

Some parents might explain in great detail to the child what it is she is doing wrong, while others might be more of the 'Do as I say, not as I do' school. Some parents might have different gender expectations, allowing boys to be more vigorous and active, and expect girls to adopt more passive pursuits.

You, the parents and the children need to know what behaviour is expected in the family. This will vary from family to family, and what works in one case may not in another. What remains true is that all children have to know how far they can go before their behaviour becomes unacceptable.

CASE STUDY

Sally cares for two children. Her employer asked to look after another child during the school holidays, as her mother worked full time. She found six-year-old Clara to be a delightful child, always happy and helpful, but her habit of never saying 'Please' and 'Thank you' drove her to distraction. It was clear that this was not expected of her at home.

1 What action should Sally take?
2 Should she insist that Clara says 'Please' and 'Thank you'?

Factors that influence behaviour

Most of the factors that influence behaviour are family-based. This is because behaviour is learnt initially in the family, and the earliest experiences have the greatest effect. These factors include:

- birth order
- siblings
- expectations of the parents
- cultural child-rearing practices
- influence of the extended family
- opportunities for play within the family home
- abuse and neglect
- gender stereotyping
- domestic violence.

Outside events that affect the whole family may also influence behaviour. These might include:

- unemployment/work pattern of the parent(s)
- moving house
- divorce and separation
- adapting to a re-constituted family
- death and grieving for people and pets
- disability within the family
- winning the lottery
- continual change of caregivers.

Other factors are:

- the personality of the child
- the school
- the peer group
- the media
- having a disability
- experiencing discrimination
- being gifted.

Common causes of challenging behaviour

Some forms of behaviour are so common that one might be concerned if a child did not at occasionally display one or more of them. Some of these behaviours are due to frustrated emotional needs.

EMOTIONAL CAUSES

Attention-seeking behaviour is one of the most common forms of challenging behaviour. Children need to be reassured that they are loved and cared for. If they are not given attention, they will seek it by being aggressive, angry, rude, swearing, showing off, dominating conversations, and other negative behaviours.

Celia, an experienced nanny, has been recently employed to care for a four-year-old girl, Edwina, whose parents have recently separated. This is the third week she has been looking after her, and she is finding it very difficult to manage her constant attention-seeking behaviour. She is defiant and disobedient, frequently upsets the other children at playgroup, swears and refuses to join in any planned activities.

1 Why might she be behaving like this?
2 How might you raise this with your employer?
3 How would you help Edwina?

Temper tantrums

About half of two-year-olds have tantrums on a regular basis, usually in the presence of their parents or nanny, and very seldom when on their own or when at school or playgroup. The tantrums come about because they feel frustrated and need to get attention. Tantrums can be quite disturbing to observe, and need to be dealt with in the same way by you and the parents. If you see one coming, it is often possible to distract or divert the child, and by leaving the room you remove the main focus of the anger. If it is already too late, or you are in a public area and unable to walk away, you will need to hold and hug the child until the tantrum is over. The child will be frightened and will need reassurance.

When the tantrum is over, cuddling the child and talking about feelings in a positive way should discourage further tantrums. It is positively harmful to slap or handle a child roughly during a tantrum, and even more dangerous to shake her. Equally, giving in to the child and allowing her to manipulate you will increase the frequency of the tantrums. Always report back to parents if the child has had a severe tantrum, so that you both can follow the same consistent approach.

Jealousy
It is an unusual household that never quarrels, and most children will fight from time to time. A new baby will sometimes arouse deep feelings of jealousy from a displaced older child, and this may be shown by aggressive behaviour to the younger children. Often, rivalry is expressed by quarrelling over toys and attention. In general, children can sort out most of these rows for themselves and unless they are doing serious damage to each other, it is often better to just let them get on with it.

CASE STUDY

Susie, a newly qualified nanny is looking after a two-year-old toddler and a four-month-old baby. She was worried when, during her first week, she walked into the room to find the toddler pinching the baby, and then telling Susie to send it away.
1 Is this normal behaviour?
2 How should Susie respond to the situation:
   (a) immediately
   (b) in the long term?

Comfort behaviour
There are many forms of comfort behaviour, some more embarrassing than others. No one minds if a child drags a soft toy everywhere with her, but masturbating in public is not acceptable. Sucking thumbs, dummies, and pieces of material are all objects that children use to comfort themselves. They may become reliant on them at particular times of the day, usually at nap time and when confronted by a new or distressing situation. Not all children feel the need for a comfort object, but if a child has a comfort habit you will have to tolerate it. It would be most upsetting for the child to have the object or the habit taken away suddenly and she will give it up in her own good time.

   Other children might show their need for love and reassurance by displaying anxiety or fear, and/or withdrawn behaviour, finding it difficult to express their feelings in the usual attention seeking ways. Children need approval from adults, so as to believe that they are valued. If this is not forthcoming, their self-esteem will be low, and they will find it difficult to learn and achieve.

PHYSICAL CAUSES

Sometimes challenging behaviour has a physical cause. Lack of sleep can lead to irritability. Hunger can cause some children to lose concentration and become aggressive because their blood sugar level drops. Infection, particularly in the incubation period, can cause changes in behaviour patterns.

Some conditions, such as Asperger's syndrome, are not immediately diagnosed, but can contribute significantly to unacceptable behaviour. If you find the behaviour of a child extremely difficult to manage, it would be wise to ask the parents to find out if there is a physical cause.

GROWING INDEPENDENCE

Some types of behaviour which can be challenging are inevitable, as they are part of the child's development.

Curiosity and exploration

As a baby becomes a toddler there will not be a cupboard that remains unexplored or a meal that is peaceful and without a messy end, as the toddler seeks to feed herself and enjoy the texture as well as the taste of food. Safety factors and constant vigilance are of increasing importance as the child's curiosity knows no bounds.

Toilet training

There is much written about the best way to satisfactorily toilet train a child, and there are many myths about the time it takes and the best way to go about it. Encourage the parents not to get into any competition with any of their friends.

It is also important that you and the child's parents share the same ideas and go about the process in the same way. There is no point in you leaving the nappy off and offering the child the pot at regular intervals if the parents decide not to do this when you are having your time off. The child will just get confused. Whatever regime you choose, you must make sure that you do not adopt a punitive approach to any occasional accident. Show pleasure in any new achievement.

Activity

Thinking about all the children that you know, note down your answers to the following.
1 At what ages did the children become reliably dry and clean?
2 Was there a gender difference?
3 Was there a variation in methods used?
4 Did any parent ever suggest a regime that you felt uncomfortable with?
5 How did you manage this situation?

Dressing and undressing

Some children would always prefer to dressed by you rather than having to bother for themselves, but the majority express their independence at a young age, first by undressing and then by starting to dress themselves. It can be difficult to encourage children to dress themselves when you are in a hurry to get them ready to go out. Some children are more reluctant to dress themselves than others, but at some point they have to learn for themselves or be shown up when they start school or go to stay with a friend.

BOREDOM

Children need stimulation and the opportunity to play and learn about the world around them. If they are restricted and frustrated, this will lead to boredom, perhaps resulting in attention-seeking behaviour.

Managing unwanted behaviour

When a child is cared for by more than one person, the child will sometimes attempt to play one adult off against another, so it is helpful if both nanny and parents follow similar approaches. Consistency of care and methods of discipline help the child to know what is expected and acceptable. All children need to understand boundaries.

Toddlers, in particular, can be contrary, as they are learning what the boundaries are and what type of behaviour is encouraged. If they are given attention when they are behaving in an unacceptable way, they will repeat the behaviour. For example, if they are refused a packet of sweets, respond with a tantrum and are then given the sweets, they will have learnt that tantrums bring rewards. Your understanding of age-appropriate behaviour and developmental norms will help you to set the boundaries and to make the correct response to any challenging behaviour. Try to avoid confrontations over small, unimportant matters as children do not really distinguish between necessary rules for their safety and social niceties.

As children grow older, the rules may change, but consistency is still the key for managing behaviour. Disagreements can cause a great deal of friction, and it is worth spending some time, when you are first interviewed, agreeing what is acceptable behaviour and how this will be achieved.

Behaviour is not acceptable if it:

- is dangerous, hurtful or offensive to someone else
- is dangerous to the child herself
- will make the child unwelcome or unacceptable to other people
- damages other people's property.

CASE STUDY

Candice overhears Emily, the six-year-old in the family making a hurtful remark to Anna, her four-year-old sister, calling her 'thick and stupid'. Anna bursts into tears and hides under the table.

1   What should be Candice's first response?
2   Should she discuss this with the parents?
3   What steps might Candice take to alter such behaviour?
4   How should she support Anna?

Acceptable behaviour will be encouraged by you and the parents by:

- talking freely and frequently about the children
- discussing which rules are more flexible than others
- not allowing a child to manipulate either of you, by playing one off against the other
- treating each child as an individual. One of the children might dissolve into tears from a cross look, while another might find even a stern telling-off quite amusing
- remembering that rules should change as children become more mature, and are able to understand the effects of their behaviour.

Your role with the children is to:

- be fair
- be consistent
- have as few rules as possible
- set clearly defined boundaries, helping them to understand how far they can go and what behaviour is not acceptable
- understand what behaviour is appropriate for each age group
- have realistic expectations
- give brief explanations as to why you do not accept certain behaviours
- maintain communication and discussion with the parents
- prepare children to play a valuable role in society
- understand the different expectations that some families might have.

GOOD PRACTICE IN INFLUENCING BEHAVIOUR

1 Show approval when children behave well. Give rewards of hugs, smiles, praise, time to talk and play, and attention.
2 Praise children to their parents and other people.
3 Help children by being positive. For example, say 'Lets tidy up' rather than, 'Don't make a mess'.
4 Give children plenty of warning before it is time to tidy up.
5 Explain why you expect certain behaviours.
6 Avoid creating confrontations and battles. Do not over-react to minor matters.
7 Give children a chance to work out minor disputes. Do not intervene too soon.
8 Be firm and do not give into whining or tantrums.
9 Be a good role model. Behave in the way you wish the children to behave.

MODIFYING BEHAVIOUR

Behaviour modification is the name given to techniques used to influence and change children's behaviour. It works by promoting and rewarding positive aspects of children's behaviour and by ignoring and discouraging negative aspects. There is a spectrum of behaviour modification techniques, from the practice of firmly holding autistic children so as to force interaction upon them, to the frequent giving of praise and encouragement for 'good' behaviour.

1   Distract the child by providing more attractive alternatives.
2   Remove the child from the situation. Do not humiliate her or shut her away on her own.
3   If a child is having a tantrum, restrain her gently until she calms down, and then cuddle her and offer reassurance.
4   If there is danger, grab the child and say, 'No'!
5   Ignore swear words.
6   When you are saying 'No', make sure your whole body shows that you mean it.
7   Do not reward unacceptable behaviour with your attention.
8   Do not argue with a child in a tantrum.
9   Show disapproval, and make it clear that the behaviour is not acceptable.
10 Make it clear that it is the *behaviour* that is not wanted, rather than the child.
11 If the child is old enough to understand, explain why the behaviour is unacceptable.
12 Limit punishments, but any sanctions used must be immediate and appropriate.
13 Never smack, shake, bite or humiliate a child.
14 After any incident, show affection, and offer cuddles.
15 Stay calm and in control of yourself.

Issues that cause conflict

We all want children to eat well, go to bed on time, and live in peace with their siblings and peers, but mealtimes, nap times and sharing toys and space can all cause conflict and ignite challenging behaviour. Occasionally, nannies and parents can have conflicting views about managing these situations.

MEALTIMES

Because you will invest a great deal of care and thought in what you provide for children to eat, you may take the rejection of such food personally, and react to food refusal. This reaction and over-anxiety on the behalf of the adult gives the child power, and may encourage later food disorders.

Sensible rules as to when and where food is eaten need to be kept by both you and the parents. Agreement about the type of food provided, how it is cooked and presented, the size of the portion, second helpings, and the time allowed to eat the food all have to be sorted out before you take up the post, and up-dated as the child develops.

Table manners are personal to each family. Some families are quite happy for children to jump up and down from the table whenever they please, or to leave any food that they do not fancy that day, or to create battleships and oceans from their sausages, mash and gravy. Other families might insist on the children remaining at the table, not speaking with their mouths full, becoming dextrous with their knives and forks and acquiring social skills at any early age.

You will need to be clear about the parents' expectations so that you can reinforce them as far as possible. You will need to be a good role model for the children. Meals are social occasions, a time for conversation and exchanging the news of the day. Setting the table in an attractive way, and allowing the children to help in preparing the meal and serving the food will encourage them to value the time spent at the table. They should also be encouraged to help you clear away.

REST TIME

If a child has a regular rest time, and the parents want you to keep to this, you will need to discuss it with them. The difficulties are:
■ a child who becomes very tired and fractious needs a nap, even if the parents request that this does not take place
■ a child might not want to rest, but the parents wish her to, so that they can enjoy her company in the evening
■ the amount of rest a child needs changes as the child grows older.

SWEARING

Children are excellent mimics, and enjoy new words. They get a great deal of pleasure in repeating words that get a response. The best way to deal with swearing is to ignore it. This could cause conflict if the parents are repeatedly correcting a child who swears or, on the other hand, if the parents swear a great deal themselves which offends you.

MASTURBATION

Some children masturbate as a comfort habit, particularly when bored, watching television or settling to sleep. The best advice is to ignore it, particularly in the younger child. Older children will soon learn from their peers that masturbating in public is unacceptable. Older people, such as grandparents, might find masturbating hard to ignore. If this behaviour is upsetting to anyone, it is often possible to distract the child, by offering them something new and exciting to do.

When children's behaviour causes concern, you need to question whether this is a normal stage in their development or a more serious problem. Most problems sort themselves out in time, and even the most quarrelsome child can become charming and manageable. If this is not the case, you may have to encourage the parents to seek other professional help.

The smacking debate

Smacking is a negative way of dealing with behaviour problems, as the main thing the child learns is that larger people can hurt them, and when they grow up they will be able to hurt smaller people. It seldom resolves the problem.

If parents smack their children (and the UK is one of the last European countries where it is legal to do so) it may be harder for you to correct their behaviour by other means. As a professional person looking after other people's children, it is never correct to administer physical punishment whether the parents request it or not. A light slap is one end of the continuum of beating a child and causing injury, and there would never be any reason why a nanny should hit a child. In your working career, you may come across parents who choose to use physical chastisement to discipline their children. You must use your judgement as to when you feel it is necessary to intervene. Parents sometimes need help in understanding there are alternative modes of control.

Activity
As a nanny, how might you manage the following situations?
1   An older child deliberately provokes his younger brother into losing his temper and throwing food onto the floor.
2   A three-year-old refuses to rest, although obviously very tired.
3   A three-year-old refuses to put on his coat to go outside in very cold weather.
4   A six-year-old taunts and teases children from a different family.
5   A child demands sweets in a supermarket.
6   Three children quarrel and fight in a car while you are driving.

If you have cared for a child from babyhood, it is unlikely that you will experience too many difficulties in managing her behaviour. It may be more challenging to start to care for an older child. With very few exceptions, all children respond to affectionate care in a secure consistent environment, where it is obvious that they feel loved and secure.

10 THE NEEDS OF THE YOUNG BABY

> **This chapter includes:**
> - **Understanding the demands of babies**
> - **Sharing care with parents**
> - **Routines**
> - **The development of the small baby and the need for stimulation**

Some nannies adore babies, and this may be one of the reasons they become nannies. Caring for babies is something they enjoy and are competent at providing the consistent care and stimulation that all babies need. Other nannies will see babies as too much of a responsibility and lacking the challenge of working with older children.

Understanding the demands of babies

Babies are attractive and provide their carers with constant rewards. A baby who is loved and given as much attention as she demands will reciprocate with smiles and cuddles. Caring for babies takes much time and energy. Routines have to be established, such as feeding, winding, rest times, play times, and changing and disposing of napkins. If the baby is prone to colic she will be difficult to settle, and you may have to walk around with her while you are managing your other commitments. Every time you leave the house, you will need to take a great deal of equipment with you, such as nappies, food, toys, and clothes. Small babies are very vulnerable to infection, and in addition to sterilising any feeding equipment, you will need to be extremely vigilant in preventing cross-infections.

A calm and equitable temperament helps when looking after very small babies, as they can be trying. A baby who continually cries for no apparent reason can be an upsetting and frustrating experience if all your efforts to pacify her are fruitless. If you find you are reaching the end of your tether, as an experienced nanny you will know to place the baby somewhere safe, and to remove yourself from the situation until you feel able to cope once more.

As the child matures and becomes mobile, you will have to provide close supervision throughout the day. As the child explores her environment, you will have to make sure she is safe, and try to protect your belongings and those of the older children. A baby is very messy, with her food and with play materials, and it requires patience to allow her to explore.

BUILDING A RELATIONSHIP WITH THE BABY

A baby will show her personality from the start. She may be placid or excitable, easy or difficult to feed or to settle for sleep, need constant attention or be content on her own, she may cry rarely or a great deal or may display a mixture of all of these behaviours.

Some babies appear not to mind who handles and cares for them and will welcome new people and new experiences. This makes it easier for the parent to share the care with you, knowing that the baby will be happy as long as her needs are met. Other babies are slower and more reluctant to accept change and have to be coaxed until they are more familiar with a new carer. A few babies are extremely difficult and will protest loudly at every change. Many babies will exhibit a mixture of these responses.

With a small baby, it is important that you and the mother care for the baby together for a while, so that you can be aware of the baby's fussy moods, and be shown the best way to respond to her. Small babies need warm consistent care that promotes emotional security, and encouraging the mother to spend some time at home caring for the baby together with you will reassure the mother before she leaves you in sole charge.

It may be easier to settle a very young baby with you than one of seven months or so. At this age, babies start to miss their mothers and become very aware of strangers, and with some babies this may continue for some time. Between seven and fifteen months, babies feel 'stranger anxiety': becoming anxious in the presence of strangers and strange places; and 'separation anxiety': not wishing to be separated from the primary caregiver.

Sharing care with parents

Many parents prefer to employ nannies, rather than group care, because they want consistent, individual care for their baby in the family home. You should feel pleased that they have chosen you for what could be the start of a long relationship, stretching over many years.

You will be able to appreciate how difficult it is for many parents to separate from their babies and you will need to support them by welcoming any telephone calls during the day, and by working hard to establish a strong, trusting relationship.

Communication with parents is important whatever the age of the child you are caring for, but if you are looking after babies and toddlers it is vital. They are unable to speak for themselves and cannot tell the parents what they have achieved during the day. They are also very vulnerable to infection and ill health and any changes in appetite, behaviour, excretion or sleep pattern need to be noted by both the nanny and parent, and information should be exchanged in the morning and the evening. All these events should be noted, and the parents informed at the end of the day.

Right at the start, the mother will need to tell you how she expects you to feed the baby. If she is using formula milk, you will need to discuss the making up of the feeds. If the mother is breast-feeding, she may wish to return home during the day to feed the baby and you may wish to store some frozen expressed breast milk for emergency use. This will keep for up to forty-eight hours in a fridge, or up to three months in a freezer. You will know not to use a microwave to thaw or warm milk, as it heats the milk unevenly, and it may scald the baby's mouth. As the baby matures, her feeding needs will change, and you and the mother will have to work together in introducing new tastes and foods to the baby.

You will also need to find out about the baby's preference for sleeping times and routines and comfort objects. You will need to discuss what type of nappies the mother prefers, and make sure that you always have enough in stock. The mother will also wish to tell you about the baby's skin care.

CASE STUDY

Michele looks after Peter, aged four months. She is happy in the family and has a really nice room. Cheryl, Peter's mother, works long hours, and is often not home until eight o'clock. She always wakes Peter up when she comes in so as to give him a cuddle and spend a little time with him. She then hands him over to Michele to settle him down again, and this is not always easy. Michele often misses seeing her favourite 'soap' programme on TV, and feels that if Cheryl wakes him up, then she should settle him down again.

1   Is Cheryl behaving fairly?
2   Should Michele discuss the situation with Cheryl?
3   What do you think might be the best solution?

Routines

Before leaving the baby with you, the mother will have established certain routines with her baby. It is important that these are discussed, and an attempt is made to continue the established routines.

CARE OF THE SKIN

There are some very common skin conditions that are not infectious but nevertheless need careful handling. To prevent cradle cap, heat rash, and nappy rash make sure that you and the mother:
- wash baby's hair only once or twice a week and rinse it very thoroughly
- look out for any crust on the scalp, and apply olive oil to the crust, washing it off after a few hours
- do not allow the baby to become too hot by over-dressing her, or leaving her in a hot room with a great many bed coverings
- change nappies frequently and wash the baby's bottom at each change
- are aware that creams and washing powders can cause allergies
- adequately rinse terry towelling nappies, if used
- expose the baby's skin to the air at regular intervals during the day.

BATHTIME

Bathing the baby should be an enjoyable, rewarding and relaxing time, but you need to be fully aware of the following safety measures:

- the bath should not be too full
- the cold tap should be run before the hot tap
- the temperature should be checked before putting the baby into the bath
- a non-slip mat should be put in the bath
- the baby should be put in at the end without the taps
- the room should not be cold
- all equipment should be gathered together before the bath
- the baby should never be left unattended in the bath.

Bathtime should be fun and an opportunity for the baby to splash, make bubbles, play with bath toys, enjoy the sensation of the warm water against her skin and the freedom of playing without clothes on. If the baby should be frightened of the water do not have a confrontation. It is better for the baby to go without bathing for a while until she is ready to enjoy it. Developing a fear of water as a baby could inhibit learning to swim at a later date.

SLEEP

Sleeping patterns vary considerably in babies. You need to ask the mother the baby's pattern, and understand the importance of allowing the baby to sleep when she wants to and not when it is most convenient for you. You will probably want to check on her once or twice during her nap. A baby-recording device is a useful investment.

Other safety factors include making sure that:

- cots and prams meet British Standard Institute safety regulations, displaying the Kite mark
- the mattress is firm and well fitting
- pillows and duvets are not used
- cot bumpers are avoided
- the baby is not put down to sleep if she is wearing anything with a string or ribbon round her neck.

You will soon know the amount of noise the baby can tolerate, and whether loud sudden noises disturb her or not. As the baby grows and matures, other routines such as tooth brushing and story time will be established and sleep time will be shorter.

Sudden Infant Death Syndrome (SIDS)

This is the sudden and unexpected death of an infant, usually found dead in her cot or pram with no obvious cause. It occurs in babies between the ages of one week and two years, peaking at three months and it occurs more frequently in the winter months. It has been linked with smoky environments, untreated minor ailments, over-concentrated formula feeds, and multiple births. To reduce the risk:

- always place the baby on her back in the cot or pram
- always place in the feet-to-foot position in the cot or pram, so that the baby cannot slip down under the covers
- avoid over-heating. Use blankets, not duvets, and av oid cot bumpers
- be sure to report any minor ailment to the parent.

Recent research has show that babies who died from SIDS (a small sample of 32 babies under seven months) were more likely to have been infected with helicobacter pylori, a gut bacterium transferred from the mouths or hands of other people. It is therefore not good practice to lick a dummy before replacing it in the baby's mouth, or to insert a finger in her mouth to comfort her.

PREVENTION OF INFECTION

Small babies are very vulnerable to infection and you must be scrupulous in your personal hygiene when sterilising feeding equipment, making up formulae, changing and disposing of nappies and bathing baby. If you have older children in your care, they need to be taught to always wash their hands after using the lavatory, before eating or preparing food. They should also wash their hands before handling the baby and any cuts on their hands need to be covered.

Crowds and over-heated rooms might expose the baby to the risk of illness, whereas a brisk walk in the park will only expose her to fresh air. As the baby develops and becomes more sociable and meets more people, she will be more exposed to possible infection, but by this time her immune system is more able to cope with it.

BREAST FEEDING

After a baby is born, mothers have to decide whether to breast feed or bottle feed their babies. Both have advantages and disadvantages. It is very important that the baby's food needs are met, as the first year of life is a time of very rapid growth and development. A baby who is not getting enough food may suffer development delay and restricted growth, resulting in failure to thrive.

Mothers returning to work may wish to continue to breast feed either by expressing milk, or returning home during the day. The desire to do this must be respected, but it can be stressful for everyone, as babies do not necessarily match timetables or recognise lunch breaks. Mothers should be asked to make sure there is plenty of expressed breast milk in the freezer, for you to use in an emergency.

Bottle feeds

Formula milk is usually made from cow's milk, where the protein and fat levels have been altered and vitamins and minerals added. An approximate guide to calculating the amount of formula milk required by a baby is 75 ml of fully re-constituted feed for every 500 g of a baby's weight (two and a half fluid ounces per pound body weight) in twenty-four hours. The total is divided into the num-ber of bottles the baby is likely to take in that time. Like a breast-fed baby, the baby should be allowed to dictate its feeding requirements to allow for changes in appetite and growth.

Studies have shown that bottle fed babies are frequently given feeds that are over- or under-concentrated, so always read and follow the instructions on the packet, as manufacturers often develop and change their products. See page 140 for how to prepare a bottle feed.

All equipment (bottles, teats, bottle tops, scoops) used for bottle-feeding should be sterile as germs thrive on milk. Sterilisation of this equipment usually involves using a chemical agent such as Milton™, for keeping bottles free from germs that cause disease (see page 141). Bottles and equipment may also be boiled, but have to be kept under the boiling water for at least ten minutes. You should always make sure you have washed your hands before preparing bottles.

Apart from making completely sure that the feed is germ free, it is equally important to know how to hold the baby when giving a feed. Both the adult and the baby need to be comfortable and to look at each other, and the adult should speak softly and encouragingly to the baby from time to time. Never leave the baby on her own with a bottle (prop feeding), as this is very dangerous as the baby might choke.

WEANING

It is recommended that babies should be weaned (introduced to solid food) between the ages of four and six months (see page 141), by which age the baby's digestive system is more able to cope with a variety of food. The milk diet alone might not be satisfying a baby, and she might be waking up hungry during the night.

1 Check that the formula has not passed its sell-by date. Read the instructions on the tin. Ensure the tin has been kept in a cool, dry cupboard.

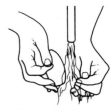

2 Boil some **fresh** water and allow to cool.

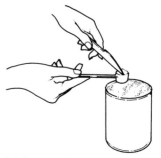

3 Wash hands and nails thoroughly.

4 Take required equipment from sterilising tank and rinse with cool, boiled water.

5 Fill bottle, or a jug if making a large quantity, to the required level with water.

6 Measure the **exact** amount of powder using the scoop provided. Level with a knife. **Do not pack down.**

7 Add the powder to the measured water in the bottle or jug.

8 Screw cap on bottle and shake, or mix well in the jug and pour into sterilised bottles.

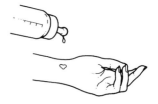

9 If not using immediately, **cool quickly** and store in the fridge. If using immediately, test temperature on the inside of your wrist.

10 Babies will take cold milk but they prefer warm food (as from the breast). If you wish to warm the milk, place bottle in a jug of hot water. **Never keep warm for longer than 45 minutes** to reduce chances of bacteria breeding.

Note Whenever the bottle is left for short periods, or stored in the fridge, cover with the cap provided.

Preparing the bottle feed

1 Wash the bottles, teats and other equipment in hot water and detergent. Use a bottle brush for the inside of bottles. **Do not rub salt on the teats.** Squeeze boiled water through the teats.

2 Rinse everything thoroughly in clean running water.

3 Fill the steriliser with clean, cold water. Add chemical solution. If in tablet form, allow to dissolve.

4 Put the bottles, teats and other equipment (nothing metal) into the water. Ensure everything is covered completely by the water, with no bubbles. If necessary, weight down. Leave for the required time according to manufacturer's instructions.

Sterilising feeding equipment

By six months, the baby's reserves of iron that she took in during the pregnancy have run out, and milk on its own does not provide enough for her. She will need some iron rich foods such as lentils, apricots and green leaf vegetables. For the first two weeks, just one teaspoonful of pureed vegetables a day is enough. This should be offered after a feed as she is less likely to refuse it.

For the next six to eight weeks, gradually introduce solids three times a day before, during or after milk feeds. These first solid foods should be soft and lump free (pureed), as the baby cannot chew and finds it difficult to swallow and digest lumps.

For the baby of six months, solid food becomes important for growth and the prevention of anaemia. From this age, the baby can hold foods (finger foods) and food that is no longer pureed but just mashed may be introduced. Finger foods could include pieces of carrot and apple, crusts of bread or rice biscuits. It is also thought that if solid food is not introduced by six months an important developmental stage may be missed, resulting in chewing difficulties and food refusal. Babies should have their own plate and spoon. This equipment does not have to be sterilised, but should be kept very clean.

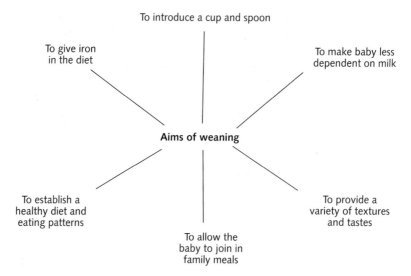

To introduce a cup and spoon

To give iron
in the diet

To make baby less
dependent on milk

Aims of weaning

To establish a
healthy diet and
eating patterns

To provide a
variety of textures
and tastes

To allow the
baby to join in
family meals

Aims of weaning

The first foods should not have salt or sugar added to them, as the kidneys cannot digest salt, and too much sugar can lead to a craving for sweet food and eventual tooth decay. Any cereal containing gluten (a protein found in cereals, such as wheat, barley, oats and rye) should be avoided until the baby is at least seven months, as there is a danger of allergy to gluten.

Eggs that are well cooked can be introduced towards the end of the first year. Never give soft-boiled eggs to a baby because of the risk of salmonella food poisoning. After six months, as the quantity of solid food is increased, the amount of milk offered may be gradually reduced. The fluid should be replaced with cooled boiled water, given in a cup.

All mealtimes, especially those for a baby, should take place in a quiet calm atmosphere. New tastes should be encouraged without ever forcing them upon her. If the baby dislikes something on a Monday, she may well enjoy it the following Friday. It is always worthwhile re-introducing foods, as the baby's tastes become more mature. Babies should be encouraged to enjoy their food, allowed to help by holding a spoon, given finger foods, and no fuss should be made if there is any mess.

HEALTH CHECKS

Once the mother has returned to work, it is possible that she will ask you to take the baby to the clinic for her regular developmental, hearing and health checks and for her immunisations. Written permission will be needed before the immunisations can be given, and the doctor will wish to have a full medical history, which only the parents can provide. If there are any anxieties about the baby's development or health, the parent will wish to attend the clinic. The health visitor's name and number will be recorded on the medical information chart and it may be useful to establish a relationship with her.

The development of the small baby and the need for stimulation

Babies are learning and developing as soon as they are born, quickly learning to recognise the smell, taste, voice, feel and face of the mother, thus using all the senses to ensure survival. In addition to love, protection, shelter and food the baby also needs stimulation. At first the mother provides all the stimulation the baby requires through gentle handling and stroking, speaking in a soft voice and feeding. As the baby develops, the interaction between the mother or the main caregiver and the baby becomes increasingly important. As routines become established, there is time to play when feeding, bathing and changing nappies. Many babies are spending longer parts of the day awake, and you will have fun interacting and playing with her and making sure that she is not left alone or bored.

ENCOURAGING DEVELOPMENT

By six weeks, most babies are smiling, showing that they are responding to a stimulus, usually during a conversation whilst maintaining good eye contact. This is a good time to introduce mobiles and rattles. The mobiles that will interest her most will have horizontal pictures, so that she can gaze at them when lying on her back in a cot, or supported in a bouncing cradle. Bright colours add interest and some mobiles have a musical attachment.

Many toys are taken to the baby's mouth, so that she can learn with one of the most sensitive parts of her body the shape and substance of the object. This should not be discouraged, but checks must be made for safety. Everything needs to be durable, well made, non-toxic, with no sharp edges, washable and be too large to swallow.

By far the most important stimulus is still the consistent contact given to the baby by parents, family and nanny. Interacting with songs and cuddles and talking to the baby will aid emotional, cognitive and language development. The first response will be facial, smiles and intense looks. Be sure to take turns and listen to the baby when she begins to vocalise. After changing the baby's nappy allow time for her to play with hands and feet unrestricted by clothing.

At around six weeks, babies can be seen occasionally moving their hands towards objects in their field of vision and sometimes accidentally succeeding in touching them. At three months, the baby discovers her hands and begins to engage in finger play. By six months, this area of hand–eye co-ordination is usually well established and babies can reach out for a desired object and grasp it. Initially, toys such as an activity centre, which hang suspended just within the baby's reach, will help develop this skill. Play mats with a range of different sensory activities will help stimulate the baby's interest.

Increasingly, the baby's responses are no longer just reflex actions to sensory stimuli, but become selective, choosing which stimulus to react to. Lightweight rattles and toys that can be easily held in the hand help to develop hand/eye co-ordination.

Once the baby is able to sit up, supported by cushions, other toys may be offered. An exciting assortment of objects gathered together for her to explore will encourage her all-round development. Bricks can be built into towers and knocked down. Objects can be banged together. Singing to a baby comes naturally to most adults. From action songs to finger rhymes, from nursery rhymes to lullabies, the baby will get pleasure from them all and enjoy a sense of security and comfort. Singing helps babies to recognise different sounds and anticipate repetitive actions.

At this age too, your baby will start to enjoy books. Sitting with you and looking at pictures of familiar objects can start as young as six months, and will lay the foundation for a life-long enjoyment of books.

If you look after a baby from birth, you are likely to become very attached to her. This might make it difficult for you to move on, but is one of the most rewarding and fulfilling jobs a nanny can experience. If you find looking after newborn babies is what you enjoy most, you might consider registering with an agency as a maternity nurse. This usually involves just being responsible for the newborn baby, but only for a short time, generally about a month.

11 ENCOURAGING DEVELOPMENT IN THE ONE- TO FIVE-YEAR-OLD

> **This chapter includes:**
> - Encouraging development in the toddler (the one- to three-year-old)
> - Encouraging development in the pre-school child (the three- to five-year-old)

As well as the physical care of the young child, such as establishing routines and health care, an important part of your role will be to understand the developmental needs of the child, and to encourage learning.

Encouraging development in the toddler (the one- to three-year-old)

Toddlers are challenging and often the child may use the toys and activities provided by you in a very different way, but this is acceptable, as learning is still taking place. Toddlers should be given every opportunity to explore and set their own agenda within a safe environment.

Taking toddlers to the park, shopping, visiting friends, parent and toddler groups, drop-in centres, the local library and visits to the clinic where other small children are likely to be found, will enlarge her social circle and allow her to play alongside other children. Provision of small scale household equipment, such as brooms, tea-sets and telephones, promotes domestic play and the beginning of role play.

PHYSICAL DEVELOPMENT

During the first year of life, the baby will have developed physical control. Some will be walking confidently by their first birthday, while others may need encouragement to get started and develop balance and co-ordination.

If you have stairs in your home, the gate may be removed on occasion, and the toddler shown how to climb up the stairs and, more importantly, how to crawl down. Strong supermarket cartons, which are sturdy and large enough for toddlers to climb in, promote skills of getting in and out of objects, co-ordination and balance.

FINE MANIPULATIVE SKILLS

During the first year, babies start to practice handling and manipulating small objects, reaching and grasping, holding and letting go, moving objects from hand to hand, passing objects, poking and pointing with one finger, and picking up objects with finger and thumb.

Equipment and activities that aid physical skills
There are many materials that will help develop manipulative skills and hand–eye co-ordination, such as bricks for building towers that can be knocked down; stacking cups and beakers; small tins and cartons that can be improvised from around the house; posting boxes; hammer sets; dolls that are easily undressed and simple inset jigsaws. Toddlers need plenty of hands-on experience and need to repeat the play many times. They are just entering the concrete-operational stage (a stage observed and recorded by Jean Piaget), and need to handle materials in order to understand them.

Outings to parks where the playground will have swings, seesaws, climbing frames and rocking toys are enjoyable and aid balance and co-ordination as well as strengthening arm and leg muscles.

Ball play, pull-along toys and small scale climbing and sliding equipment encourage physical skills. Other toys and equipment you might find she enjoys at this age include wheeled toys to sit on and move with the feet, rockers, and tunnels and boxes to climb in and out.

The contents of the lower kitchen cupboards, where it is sensible to store only safe sturdy equipment such as saucepans, plastic storage containers, baking tins and wooden spoons, can be played with as well as small bouncy balls, Duplo™, large threading toys and screw toys. Play dough, crayons and finger paints can be used.

INTELLECTUAL DEVELOPMENT AND LANGUAGE

Children learn at an amazing rate, and during the first year the baby has learnt, among other things, to become mobile, to understand a great deal of what is said, to speak a few words, to identify people with whom she is in regular contact, and to recognise food she enjoys. The next year shows an acceleration of learning as the toddler becomes more proficient with language. Her curiosity seems endless! Any activity you set up for a toddler is unlikely to be used in the way that you expect. Do not be concerned, as she is still learning, although it might be something different than you originally intended. You should not expect a finished product when a toddler is involved in an activity; it is the process of discovery that is important to her.

The toddler spends an increasingly large proportion of time in exploratory and experimental play. She will enjoy looking at books, listening to and taking part in songs and rhymes, learning that objects have names as do parts of the body, and realising that by using language needs are met without having to point and cry. Children's minds develop at different rates and in different ways, and they often have individual preoccupations, such as wrapping things up, making 'nests' and arranging objects in straight lines over and over again.

Activity

Build up a repertoire of songs and finger rhymes to use with babies and toddlers.

The best way to promote language development is to find the time to sit down with a toddler with a book or a toy, and have an enjoyable conversation, making sure you take the time to listen to her responses, and to enlarge on her replies.

EMOTIONAL DEVELOPMENT

During the first year, the baby has progressed emotionally from total dependency to an understanding that there are some things she is able to do on her own and this increases during the second year. You will need to have patience as the toddler tries to help you with her own care, or assist with the chores. Supporting toddlers in learning to feed and dress themselves, and to become toilet trained will boost their confidence and self-esteem. Tantrums can be caused by the toddler being bored, frustrated, hot or cold, hungry or feeling anxious. Sometimes they just cannot cope with their angry feelings. It is often possible to avoid confrontations, but if these do take place toddlers are usually quite amenable to diversions. Some feelings are so strong and over-powering that you just have to wait until the storm has passed and then cuddle and comfort her, as she may well be frightened by the immensity of these emotions.

A great deal depends on the developing personality of the child as to how happy or sad she may be. Comfort objects may play a large part in her life and no attempt should be made to remove them. It is best to have as few rules as possible and to make sure that the environment is safe and offers security. Toddlers still need the love and support of a familiar adult and find new emotional demands difficult to deal with. You need to be aware of this when first building a relationship with a child of this age and proceed slowly and sensitively.

SOCIAL DEVELOPMENT

During the second year as the child begins to understand more, she has to learn how to fit happily into the household and the larger outside environment and a whole set of rules has to be learnt about acceptable behaviour. At this stage, play is solitary, but the presence of a familiar adult provides reassurance and security. The toddler is not interested in playing co-operatively with other children. She has just learnt the meaning of 'mine', and the concept of sharing does not usually occur until the third year. During this year, it is important to encourage play with other toddlers so as to encourage her social skills.

SENSORY DEVELOPMENT

Very young children learn mainly through their senses. As they grow older, learning in this way becomes less dominant. Toddlers, not yet in full command of

language, use all their senses spontaneously in exploratory and experimental play. In general, toddlers will explore everything through the senses as this is instinctive, but you may need to encourage children who have some sensory impairment.

Many children will attend special activity classes such as swimming, gym, creative art and music. Other sessions may be mostly social, where children get the opportunity to play with others of a similar age while their carers may enjoy meeting each other.

Encouraging development in the pre-school child (the three- to five-year-old)

By the age of three, most children will be attending either a nursery or a pre-school. Three- and four-year-olds are generally happy outgoing little people, who enjoy life and want to please adults and get on with other children. Between the ages of three and five years, physical skills that were learnt previously will be improved. Skills such as hopping, skipping, crossing the legs when seated, catching and throwing balls will all be in evidence in most four-year-olds. Some four-year-olds can ride a two-wheeler bicycle, often needing stabilisers. They can climb, run and jump on one or both feet. They enjoy all physical activities, and should have the opportunity of playing outside as often as they wish so as to practise these skills.

Most pre-schoolers enjoy eating with adults, using cutlery mostly correctly, and are less fussy about their food. They can wash their hands and manage some fastenings, such as buttons, but shoe laces will probably be beyond most of them. They are able to build with construction toys, the younger ones using Duplo™ and the older ones coping with Lego™. By the time they are five, most will be able to colour in pictures within the lines and have enough control of a pencil to write their name and do recognisable drawings.

There is a spurt in intellectual development between three and five years. The five-year-old will recognise shapes, know colours, count and do basic mathematical sums, and some may even have begun to read. Their language is now fully developed, with an increasing vocabulary the more they are read and talked to. Grammatically, the language is now more correct and they are using full sentences. Most children know how old they are, and can repeat their name, address, birthday and telephone number. They understand relationships in the family. They can talk about past experiences, and retell stories. This is the time when children ask continual questions, and you will need patience to answer them satisfactorily. A sense of humour develops, and from four years much pleasure is found in jokes and nonsense rhymes.

They are full of wonder and curiosity, and usually a delight to be with. Socially, they will be friends with both boys and girls. They are friendly to adults and children alike, and some need to be taught not to run up to every stranger they meet. By the time they are five, a sense of fair play is developing, they have learnt to share and they understand rules, playing games usually in a co-operative way. They are becoming more and more independent, being able to look after their toilet needs for themselves and to dress and undress. They now choose their own friends, no longer having to rely on their parents to choose friends for them. They become upset if their friends are distressed, showing caring attitudes.

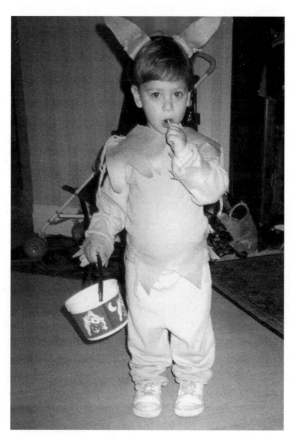

THE EARLY YEARS CURRICULUM

The curriculum can be described as the experiences, opportunities and activities that you offer children in your care, to help them to learn and develop. Some of these activities you will prepare and plan. Other opportunities for learning will occur unexpectedly and your skill will be needed to make the best use of them.

Early learning goals

For young children, the curriculum is based on a series of outcomes (early learning goals) that children will be expected to reach by the time they have completed the first year in infant school (either the reception class or the kindergarten). It must be emphasised that this is not what children are expected to do at three or even four years of age. The outcomes are organised in six areas of learning:

- personal, emotional and social development
- language and literacy
- mathematical development
- knowledge and understanding of the world
- physical development
- creative development.

Children learn from everything they do. Any activity will offer an opportunity to learn across a range of early learning goals. Everything you do with the child will contribute to the curriculum, whether it is:

- preparing and sitting down to eat a leisurely meal with the children
- involving them in domestic tasks, such as clearing up, shopping and gardening
- going for a walk in the park
- all the play activities you plan, inside and out of doors
- any routine carried out by you and the children, that you are describing and talking about with them.

Some parents may put a great deal of pressure on their children to achieve intellectually. You may have to discuss this with them if you feel this is making the children over-anxious.

Activity

Plan an outing to the supermarket with the children in your care. What contribution will this make to the six early learning goals?

All activities and experiences for children should be appropriate for their stage of development and should use as a starting point the child's current stage of development based on what the child can already do and has achieved so far, and the child's interests and preferences. Children develop at different rates and it is not helpful to compare children with one another. The learning outcomes should not be seen as the ultimate and only goals for five-year-olds. Many children of this age are capable of much more and of much wider learning.

12 THE NEEDS OF THE SCHOOL-AGE CHILD

> **This chapter includes:**
> - **Growing independence**
> - **Road safety**
> - **Liaison with the school**
> - **Bullying**
> - **Leisure activities**
> - **Changing your role**

There may well be a baby, a toddler and an older child within the family that employ you. School-age children have different needs from younger ones, but still need your care and attention before and after school and in the holidays. It is known that strong links between the home and school encourage achievement, and your role in liaising between the school and the parents is a vital one.

Growing independence

Once a child starts school full-time, she will be increasingly independent and her friends (peer group) will become more important. At five years old, most children

will be able to dress and undress themselves, clean their teeth, comb their hair, wash themselves and attend to all their toilet needs. By six or seven, they can usually make themselves a snack, skip with a rope and ride a two-wheeler bike skilfully. Ball skills develop and often take up a large part of their leisure time.

Children of five start learning to write, and this skill is developed and improved all through their school days. Tying shoelaces and colouring in without going over the lines are indicators of better control (hand–eye co-ordination).

Physical skills continue to improve and develop. Muscles become stronger and outside play can become more energetic. Team games help social development. Swimming is learnt. Regular sporting activities and exercise encourage these skills and lay down interest in later life for keeping fit and healthy.

Starting school will obviously encourage intellectual development, as the young child is keen to learn and ask many questions about events outside her family. A good school and an interested family will help to keep these interests alive throughout childhood. By eight years of age, most children will be able to read quite well, write short stories, will have some mathematical skills, tell the time and perhaps start to learn a musical instrument, act in a play, and paint and draw. Between the ages of eight and twelve children begin to think in a more abstract way. They do not need to have, for example, actual counters in front of them to calculate numbers.

Being able to think logically becomes increasingly developed throughout the school years. Their language and vocabulary is often as good as an adult's. This

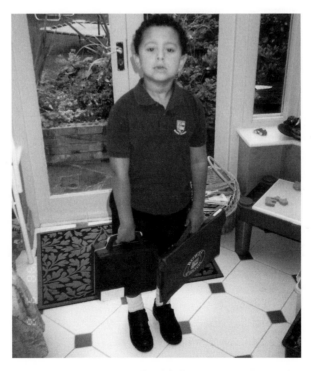

will depend to some extent on the language abilities of the family and the other adults they mix with.

Some children, when they first start school will find the noise level, the number of children, and the size of the school and the playground rather frightening at first. Their development may appear to go backwards. Having to go to the lavatory on her own may be an unpleasant experience, especially if they are not kept clean. She might become fussy about food, demand help with putting on outside clothes and play with toys that are old and familiar. This is just an adjustment to having to be a 'big girl' while at school, and a perfectly normal stage of development. A full school day is physically tiring, and this might also affect her behaviour.

On some days, she may be full of news and expect your undivided attention as she relates the exciting events of the day. At other times, perhaps after a day when things have not gone so well, she may be silent and sullen, and just want to flop down on the couch and watch the television.

At five years of age, she begins to have her own private world separate from her family. Sometimes this leads to increasing fights and squabbles with younger brothers and sisters as she needs her own privacy and a place to think.

From about the age of eight, this growing independence should be encouraged and her parents and carers need to let go gradually, trusting her to make her own mistakes within a framework of respect, and valuing her as a more independent person. School-age children become more aware of their special identity and gender, due to the influence of their friends.

KEEPING TO A ROUTINE

Children have a busy day at school, and need to have their routine firmly structured. Going to bed at a reasonable time, dressing themselves as quickly and efficiently as they can manage, having time to eat a nutritious breakfast, cleaning teeth and combing hair, and being ready on time all take practice. You can play your part in preparing the child by making sure that in the holiday before school starts she can dress and undress herself and see to all her toilet needs. You can talk to her about the school day and how it will be more structured than the pre-school. Without frightening her, you could explain that the playground will be noisier than she is used to and the dining room will be larger. The lavatories may not be as hygienic as those in the pre-school and there may not always be anyone to accompany her.

Alternatively, she could be a child new to you, whose mother has returned to work now that her daughter has started school. In this case, the child may need some additional care and attention at first, as she has to adjust to two new environments.

When collecting the child from school, you will need to make sure that she is not kept waiting. Even a few minutes left behind after the other children have left can have a very negative effect on a child. After school, she will need some time to unwind and perhaps have a snack before starting her homework or attending any extra-mural activities. It needs a fair amount of self-discipline for her to ignore the younger children who may be playing in the garden or watching television and you may have to persuade her to stick to her routine.

Communicating with the parents is just as important at this age as it was with the younger children. You will need to discuss and agree with the changing rules in the parents' household, in respect of the child's growing independence, so that you can offer the same consistent approach.

Giving her more responsibility and trusting her judgement works both ways, and you will expect her to become increasingly considerate, and adhere to the rules of the house. As she grows older, rules may have to be re-written, and agreed between the parents, the child and the nanny.

Activities
1 Describe how you might give added responsibility to older children.
2 How would you encourage school-age children to express their feelings?

You will have discussed with the child's parents the routine that is required after school. Children these days have very busy lives, full of extra-mural activities at the weekend, extra classes and coaching, parties and team games, Cubs and Brownies. You will be involved in taking and picking up children from these activities. There will be little time for organised activities at home during the school year, and there is a lot to be said for identifying some time for 'free play'.

The child's circle of friends will become increasingly important to her and her regard for their opinion will start to displace her wish to always please you or her parents. You might be told, when you arrive to collect her from school, that she has been invited to her best friend's for tea that day. Some parents might allow this, but others might expect you to explain to the friend's parent that your employers wish you to collect the child, and suggest that any social arrangements are made through the parents, giving you adequate notice. Although most families look after their child's visitors adequately, there may be some children whose family lifestyle is more haphazard, and you may feel it is safer for those children to visit you instead.

Sometimes a child's choice of friends can cause conflict. Either the parents might not like the family, or you might find the friend rude and an undesirable influence. The choice of the parents would override your feelings, but, at the end of the day, the choice of the child will dominate.

Road safety

Before the age of ten, most young children will have a different perception of speed and distance from adults, and are therefore not safe crossing roads on their own. You may be involved in taking and fetching children from school, and may have to take all the children in the family with you. Where possible, children should walk to school as this is better for their health and the environment. It also gives you the opportunity to apply the rules of road safety, teaching the children how to cross the road safely, and following the rules yourself at all times. If you are using the car, appropriate restraints will have to be fitted and used on every occasion.

There is a certain discipline the children will have to obey if they are to be totally safe when out with you. If you are caring for children of varying ages, from babies to school-age, the baby should be strapped in the harness in the pram, the toddler should wear reins, and be held firmly by you, and the older children should walk close the pram, and never be allowed to run too far ahead. When you arrive at the school, you will have to take all the children in with you and never leave the baby in the pram unattended.

Liaison with the school

The parents will have made the initial contact with the school, met the teachers and seen the classroom. Once you start to take and collect the child from the school, you will begin to make relationships with the staff team and will be informed of any concern or achievement that has taken place during the day. The school will need to understand that the parents trust you and have given you permission to discuss their child, and convey messages back to them. Some teachers find this difficult because of the professional rules of confidentiality, and you may need to take the parents' written consent. Make sure parents receive all written and practical information given to you by the school and do not rely on the children to do so – they often forget!

Activity
How might a nanny encourage teachers to accept them as professional carers and educators?

There may be times when the child becomes ill after her parents have gone to work, and you will have to make the decision about her attendance. If she becomes sick at school, you might have to collect her early and look after her. You need to have firm guidelines from the parents as to your role, and their expectations.

Most schools have outings once a term, and they depend on adult support to make these outings viable. The parents might expect you to volunteer your services.

If you are asked to help with homework, all the information the parents receive from the school about curriculum planning needs to be shared with you, so that you understand what is required. There are some practical issues, such as:
- finding a quiet place for the child to work
- agreeing with the child and the parents how much time should be given to homework
- what homework needs to be done on which night.

As this will be a very busy time of day for you, it may be difficult to offer intensive one-to-one support. Encourage the parents to share the information they receive at parents' evenings with you, so that you can further help the child.

Bullying

The child you are caring for might be unfortunate enough to be one of the number of children who are the victims of bullying. Bullying is rare among under-fives, but can occur even though they are usually well supervised at all times. In the infant school, some forms of bullying may take place, such as name calling, fighting, excluding a child from her peer group, 'sending to Coventry' and racial abuse. Bullying includes:
- deliberate hostility and violence
- a victim who is weaker than the bully
- a painful and distressing outcome for the victim.

Bullying is the main cause for school refusal and can result in emotional scars that remain for life.

CASE STUDY

Jayshree looks after children aged six, four and three years. When she collects Daniel, the six-year-old, from school he is usually very quiet and holds her hand tightly. When he came out of school on Tuesday, his coat was torn, and he had a scratch on his face. His teacher said he had had a fight with another boy. When Jayshree talks to Daniel at home, he reluctantly tells her that he hates school, and that some bigger boys are always picking on him in the playground.

1   What steps might Jayshree take to help the child in the short term?
2   How should she discuss this with the parents?
3   What sources of help might be available?

Nannies have a responsibility to tackle bullying alongside parents and teachers. If you are caring for a child who is being bullied, you will comfort and reassure the child and discuss the issue with the parents and, if the parents request it, with the school.

CASE STUDY

Sylvia, an experienced nanny, was preparing the tea in the kitchen, when she overheard David, aged seven, being racially abusive towards his friend Ashid, aged six. When David saw Sylvia, he stopped. Sylvia decided to ignore it for the time being, and planned to talk to David's mother about it when she came home.

1   Was this the right approach?
2   How could she prevent such behaviour in the future?
3   What should she do about Ashid?

Leisure activities

During school holidays, you will naturally have more contact with the older children.

Sometimes they may be booked in to play schemes or sports camps, and you would be looking after them at similar times as in term time. If not, the activities you normally provide for the pre-school children will have to be extended, and made interesting for older children. For example, if you have introduced a junk modelling activity, ask older children for their ideas for a theme and allow it to continue until the project is complete.

Most local authorities provide a range of activities and entertainment in their parks and libraries. The newspaper will also give information as to what is available. Many museums mount special interactive exhibitions for children during the holidays. It may be useful to design a large chart, displaying details of what is available for each day as a reminder of where you might take the children. Many nannies get together in the holidays, arranging outings together and pooling resources.

AFTER-SCHOOL ACTIVITIES

Many parents are keen for their children to attend after-school or weekend clubs and classes. This allows children to develop new skills, make new friends, keep fit and boost their self-esteem and confidence. The parents may leave you to make the arrangements. You will need to make sure a suitably qualified instructor holds the class. Staying at the first class will allow you to see that the children are well controlled and receiving constructive comments from the tutor. There should be a good balance between learning, fun and discipline.

It is best to let the child have some choice in the activity, as anything chosen without her knowledge is bound not to please her! The tutor should let her attend a class first on a trial basis, so that she does not have to commit herself without understanding what is expected. Be guided by the child's interests, talents and personality.

Changing your role

Some nannies grow so fond of their families that they never want to leave, even though there is less for them to do once the youngest child starts school. If this should apply to you, you would need to re-negotiate your job description. The family would probably be keen for you to be occupied during the school day, and support you in further training or in pursuing a hobby. In return, you might be expected to continue to care for the children before and after school, provide full childcare cover during the school holidays and perhaps be available for babysitting two or three evenings a week.

Some nannies, perhaps those without professional training, might stay with the family, performing a housekeeping role. As the children become more independent, those of you with qualifications will probably miss the daily contact with babies and toddlers and decide to move on.

13 THE NEEDS OF A CHILD WITH A DISABILITY

> ## This chapter includes:
> - **Defining disability**
> - **Deciding to care for a child with a disability**
> - **The needs of other children in the family**
> - **Planning suitable activities**
> - **The needs of the parents**
> - **Working with other professionals**

If you wish to care for a child who has a disability, the severity and type of the disability will determine the qualifications and level of experience that is needed to provide the specialist care that the child requires. There are agencies that specialise in providing nannies for families where there is a disabled child, such as Network Nannies, Handon Cottage, Markwick Lane, Loxhill, Godalming, Surrey, GU8 4BD (telephone: 0483 208 270) and Snap! Child Care (telephone: 020 7729 2200). Parents leaving the nanny in sole charge will see it as vitally important that they find someone they can trust to care for their child in a highly professional and competent manner.

During your career as a nanny, you may be employed to care for a child with an obvious condition, such as Down's Syndrome or cerebral palsy. You might be working with a child who has been diagnosed with delayed speech or thalassaemia. On the other hand, during the time you are working for the family, it might come to light that one of the children has a specific impairment, such as a hearing loss.

All children have the same needs: to be loved, valued, feel secure and protected, to receive routine physical care and to have enough stimulation to achieve their potential. Children with a disability may have additional needs and require extra help, but the important thing to remember is that you view the child as a person in her own right, and not just see the impairment.

Defining disability

In 1980, the World Health Organisation (WHO) defined disability as 'Any restriction or lack (resulting from impairment) of ability to perform an activity in the manner or within the range considered normal for a human being'.

Up to 20 per cent of children are estimated to have a disability of some kind. This includes children with:
- physical impairments
- sensory impairments affecting sight, speech and hearing
- a range of learning difficulties

- medical conditions such as asthma, diabetes, sickle cell, epilepsy, eczema, thalassaemia
- special diets, such as milk free, nut free, gluten free, sugar free
- behaviour and emotional difficulties, including hyperactivity
- HIV positive status
- a combination of any of the above.

Deciding to care for a child with a disability

If you are considering working with a child with a disability, there are skills, attitudes and knowledge that you need to have. You must:
- be of a calm and patient disposition
- have a good sense of humour
- be physically strong, as you may have to lift a child, or manage a child having a fit
- have a firm consistent approach, as you would with all the children
- have information from the parents as well as doing your own research, about the causes of the condition, and its possible wide-ranging effects
- be responsible for administering medication, as instructed by the parents
- be willing to undertake a short course of specialised training, if available
- be prepared to research and contact organisations
- be willing and competent to carry out necessary therapies
- be competent in using any necessary aids
- be willing to liaise with specialists, therapists and support groups
- be optimistic about the child's potential, physically and intellectually
- see the child rather than the disability.

It is useful to be computer literate and be able to access the Internet for up-to-date information.

Part of the process in deciding if you are the right person is:
- being realistic. You need a good deal of strength and stamina
- your experience in caring for disabled children, and for those without disabilities
- the specific experience of this child's condition
- knowledge of appropriate language when referring to or discussing the disability or impairment
- a willingness to learn about therapies, such as physiotherapy and speech therapy
- knowledge and maintenance of aids that might be needed
- a willingness to learn about any programmes this child might be following, and to undertake such programmes
- ideas you might have for encouraging her development
- observation skills and written records
- an awareness of her specific needs and a willingness to provide appropriate care
- communication skills with child, parents, and outside agencies.

Some common worries, apart from a general fear of the unknown, may include:

- mealtimes
- how to give enough time to all the children in the family
- how to communicate with the child
- coping with an incontinent child
- lifting the child in a skilled way
- dealing with strange patterns of behaviour
- managing a child with epilepsy.

Having a sympathetic nature is not enough. You must be sure not to over-protect the child, see that she is encouraged to reach her full potential, and be ready to support her in integrating herself with friends and family. You may be involved in an intensive training programme with the child and this is likely to forge a strong emotional bond between you. You may find yourself having to challenge the negative and discriminatory attitudes of adults and children when you take the child on an outing. Your assertiveness techniques will be invaluable here!

Parents with disabled children may need a great deal of support themselves, and you may have to set aside some time in offering them a listening ear and allowing them to express their anxieties to you. Most conditions have support and information groups, and the parents will most likely be aware of these. Any information they have should be communicated to you.

The needs of other children in the family

Apart from the disabled child, there may be other children in the family whose needs must be met. The National Children's Home report in 1995 showed that 98 per cent of 360,000 children with disabilities live with their families, and 80 per cent of these families have more than one child. It has sometimes been found that the needs of the other children in a domestic setting are not always met, as carers have to spend so much time with the one child.

Other children in the family may experience:
- anxiety, leading to disturbed sleep
- resentment and jealousy
- fear of 'catching' the condition
- teasing and isolation at school
- emotional swings, from being loving and protective, to disturbed behaviour such as regression or attention seeking.

Other children are very aware of how much time and focus is given to the needs of the disabled child, and need some special time to talk about how they feel. You will need to:
- find time to give them individual attention every day
- reassure them that they are loved and valued
- be honest with them, and give them information appropriate to their level of understanding
- encourage them to care for the disabled child as part of the routine of the day, talking to her and playing games.

CASE STUDY

Margaret cares for Lisa who is seven years old, Tom aged four years and Simon, aged six months. Simon has just been diagnosed with cystic fibrosis, and the parents are very upset. All their attention seems to be focused on the baby.

Margaret has time to spend with Tom during the day while Lisa is at school, but finds it difficult to give Lisa enough attention when the other children are there. Lisa seems withdrawn, and often bursts into tears for little or no reason.

1 How might Margaret help Lisa?
2 Should Margaret speak to her employers about her concerns?
3 Should Margaret speak to Lisa's teacher, explaining the situation?

Planning suitable activities

All children learn through play and are naturally curious. Some children may need more help and encouragement to become involved in play. It is important to have realistic expectations of the abilities of all the children in your care, but in particular it would not be good practice to expect a child with a disability to succeed at something that her impairment makes impossible. For example, to expect a hyperactive child to sit at a table concentrating on an intricate task for more than five minutes would be unrealistic. On the other hand, do not fall into the trap of expecting too little. A child with a physical impairment is likely to be just as intelligent as any other child – think of Stephen Hawking!

Your observation skills will be a key factor in deciding what activities to offer to all the children in the family, to promote and extend their development and this applies even more to a child with a disability. All children need a great deal of praise and encouragement in order to succeed and feel confident. For some children, breaking down a task into small steps may be necessary to help them succeed.

Children with disabilities particularly benefit from play with natural materials as an end product is not required and all the experiences are pleasurable and therapeutic, increasing self-esteem and confidence. Opportunities for imaginary play may require more involvement from you but are important in helping the child to express herself. Dressing-up clothes may need to be adapted.

Children enjoy and learn a great deal from using painting and drawing materials. Standing frames can be used for motor impaired children, to support them while painting. Blowing paint through a straw to make pictures develops mouth muscles and can help poor speech expression. Children with a visual impairment should be encouraged to take part in creative art activities, using many different materials. They may need to work at an unusual angle. They will benefit from tactile and fluorescent materials and textured paper. Short stubby brushes are easier to handle.

All children enjoy playing percussion instruments and those with a disability will find music and dance relaxing and soothing. There are grip pads and stands available for music making.

Computers operated by various part of the body can present learning opportunities for children with physical disabilities, allowing access to the wider world. Programmes that teach in small steps can be helpful to children with learning difficulties.

PROMOTING THE CHILD'S SELF-IMAGE

All parents hope for confident, well-adjusted children who feel good about themselves and become independent autonomous members of society. This is harder for children with a disability, and they very quickly learn to compare themselves with other children, as there are so many activities from which they are cut off and excluded. Any activities that you plan, should be accessible to all the children, at individual levels of achievement. No child should be made to feel that she could not join in because of her particular disability.

To foster a disabled child's self-esteem you will need to:

- handle her physical needs with sensitivity
- praise any achievement, however small
- offer choices where possible, and allow the child to make decisions
- be positive and not underestimate her ability
- be sensitive to her body language (this may be her main form of communication)
- break down all planned activities into small steps, so that she can achieve
- find a suitable group of children (if she is an only child) where she has the opportunity to develop her social skills and make friends
- always use positive language and challenge any inappropriate language or behaviour from other adults or children
- encourage any sign of independence, and do not over-protect the child.

Read her stories showing positive images of children with disabilities, in an empowering role. With older children, books, stories and videos showing the achievement of people who have suffered accidents or are born with a disability are helpful in encouraging a good self-image. A child who knows she is loved and valued and treated with respect will develop confidence and enjoy the company of others.

Activity
You may hear people using insulting and derogatory language about people with disabilities. Explain how you might challenge this in adults, and what approaches you might use with children.

The needs of the parents

Parents are likely to experience many negative feelings about their children's situation, such as:

- confusion and inability to cope
- anger
- guilt
- grieving for the able-bodied child that might have been
- blaming partner or in-laws
- shame and embarrassment
- fear about the future
- rejection of the child.

Parents may also experience denial and disbelief, especially if they feel that they have contributed in some way. Bringing up a child with a disability can be a tremendous strain on parents, and can be a contributory factor to marital breakdown. Some parents experience increasing isolation from their neighbours and family.

By emphasising the child's positive aspects and achievements, you can go a long way to supporting and reassuring the parents as someone outside the family who values their child. There are many people who have surmounted difficulties to achieve a great deal in later life, writing books, running support groups, being Ministers in Government and becoming the top scientist in the country.

Contacts					
	Name/ organisation	Location	Telephone number	On-going contact	Comment
Paediatrician					
Consultant/specialist					
Child psychiatrist					
Child psychologist					
Child psychotherapist					
Medical practitioner					
Health visitor					
School doctor					
Speech therapist					
Physiotherapist					
Occupational therapist					
Dietician					
Educational psychologist					
Play therapist					
Social worker					
Support teacher					
School/nursery					
Respite care					
Child development centre					
Special programme					
Voluntary organisation					
Support scheme					
Educational home visitor					

This page may be photocopied. © Nelson Thornes Ltd 2001

Working with other professionals

You will be part of a team of people who will be constantly assessing the child and coming together to support the parents, and to make plans to encourage the child to progress. Successful teamwork will lead to a good outcome.

Each member of the team will have his or her specialist knowledge to share and competencies that might be taught to other members of the team. You will get to know each and every one of them, and begin to contribute yourself.

Most children with disabilities have a wide range of contacts with health professionals, education experts, charitable organisations and social services. For someone arriving new on the scene this can seem terribly confusing and it would be a good idea to have a chart prepared for you, listing these contacts and the roles they fulfil (see page 167).

The parent will have to attend meetings with various specialists from time to time, and it will be useful for you to go on occasion, so that you get a better understanding of the work that is being done and will be able to contribute to the discussion yourself.

Caring for a child with a disability can be very hard work, but it is also fulfilling and satisfying as you support the family and see the child make progress.

14 FINANCIAL MATTERS

> ## This chapter includes:
> - **Salary**
> - **Tax and national insurance contributions**
> - **Statutory sick pay**
> - **Maternity rights**
> - **Pensions**
> - **Insurance**
> - **Car insurance and use of the car**
> - **Budgeting**

When you enter employment as a nanny, there are many things to learn about managing your money. Many of the issues discussed such as tax and insurance are complex and regulated by law. This is a brief guide to the more common issues.

Salary

It must be clearly understood before taking up employment, what your starting gross salary is, and the method of payment. Whether this is by cash, cheque or bank credit your employer is required by law to give you a monthly or weekly pay slip, notifying you of what you have earned, and detailing any deductions from your salary.

Both gross and net income is recorded. Your gross income is your annual salary, divided either by twelve months if you are paid monthly, or by fifty-two weeks, if you are on a weekly wage. The pay slip should also detail any extra payments, such as babysitting.

Your net salary is the money that you receive (take home pay) after deductions for tax, national insurance, and any other items you have agreed, such as subscriptions. It is your employer's responsibility to make the deductions, to add their national insurance contribution, and to send this regularly to the Collector of Taxes. These amounts should be shown on the payslip. It is sensible to file the payslips away carefully as you may need them as proof of income if you later apply for benefits or for a loan. Payslips offer reassurance that your employer is deducting tax and national insurance on your behalf.

The employers are also expected to administer arrangements for statutory sick pay and statutory maternity pay. You are expected to complete a tax return for the tax office when required, usually once a year.

Salaries for nannies have risen a great deal during the last two years, and this trend looks likely to continue as more parents return to work and can afford to pay a good wage. The *Nursery World*'s monthly supplement *Professional Nanny* publishes an annual pay survey in January each year. The 2000 survey showed that the average wage for a non-residential nanny is £22,000 a year in central London. Non-residential nannies outside of London and the Home Counties earn on average £15,000 a year. Asking for a pay rise may be difficult so it is sensible to ask to have an annual review of salary included in your contract.

NATIONAL MINIMUM WAGE (NMW)

From April 1999, all employers in the UK must pay a national minimum wage rate to their employees. Currently, the minimum wage is £3.70 per hour for people of 22 years and over, and £3.20 per hour for people 18 to 21 years. This applies to all workers' gross earnings and to all actual working time. It does not cover absences for sickness or holidays. Your payslip should indicate your NMW figure and information confirming that you have received the NMW. Employers can be prosecuted if they fail to pay NMW or fail to keep accurate records.

At the moment, this does not apply to residential nannies, but they are in general paid about the NMW and many of their living costs such as heating, lighting, food and laundry are paid by their employer.

WORKING TIME REGULATIONS (WTR)

All employees in the UK are legally entitled to four weeks paid holiday a year, which can include Bank Holidays. Nannies working part-time have a pro-rata entitlement.

Nannies are also legally entitled to rest breaks during the week and during the day. You should have a rest period of 11 consecutive hours between each working day and of 24 hours in each seven-day period. This can be averaged out over two weeks.

PANN produce some excellent fact sheets on NMW and WTR that should help to make these matters clearer for you. A free booklet *A Guide to Working Time Regulations* is available from the Department of Trade and Industry (telephone: 0845 6000 925).

Overtime

The hours you are expected to work should be clearly stated on your contract, but nevertheless there will be times when you will expected to work extra hours. This could be because of a family emergency or an unexpected social engagement, but in most cases you would hope to be given some notice, and your agreement sought. Before this happens it is important that you know how this overtime is to be accounted for, either financially rewarded, or time off in lieu.

Tax and national insurance contributions

The Inland Revenue states clearly that whether you work full time or part time, residential or daily, permanent or temporary as a nanny, you are NOT SELF-EMPLOYED. The family employs you, and they are liable and legally responsible for deducting tax and national insurance contributions from your salary.

INCOME TAX

This is a tax payable by everyone on annual income. You can send for leaflets from the Inland Revenue to help you understand how your tax code is assessed. Your employer is responsible for deducting tax from your gross salary, making returns to the Inland Revenue every three months, and informing you on your pay slip the amount that has been deducted. You are entitled to request the PAYE number from your employer and any information about your pay records that you require. This information will allow you to check that your tax and national insurance payments are being paid to the Inland Revenue.

At the end of the tax year, usually in April, your employer is required by law to issue you with a P60 statement, showing your total pay and deductions for the tax year. It is sensible to take a copy and keep both the original and the copy stored safely. If you leave, for whatever reason, your employer must give you a P45 showing your PAYE code, your total earnings so far in the tax year, and how much tax you have paid since the start of the tax year. It is very important that you have this to pass on to your new employer, as otherwise you may pay more tax than required. There are Tax Offices and Tax Enquiry Centres where you may seek advice. To find your nearest office, look under 'Inland Revenue' in your local telephone book.

The tax situation for those nannies doing a nanny share is simplified if one person is the named employer and agrees to deal with all the tax and national insurance issues. For those nannies holding down two jobs, each employer would set up their own PAYE schemes. Many employers now use companies such as Nanny Tax and Nanny Payroll Service to help them with the paper work.

NATIONAL INSURANCE CONTRIBUTIONS

Your national insurance number (NI) is your unique reference, which you will keep all your life. An NI card is sent to every young person just before they reach their sixteenth birthday. It looks like a plastic credit card, and has your number printed on it. If you do not have your number contact your local Benefits Agency Office. Anyone over sixteen working and earning at a certain level has to pay these contributions, to ensure that you are entitled to unemployment benefit, maternity allowance, incapacity benefit and, eventually, basic retirement pension. Your employer has by law to make a statutory contribution. It is the employer's responsibility to pay both contributions through the PAYE scheme. If you have any concern over this, you can get a statement from the Contributions Agency, Longbenton, Newcastle upon Tyne, NE98 1YX. **If you accept cash in hand as payment you would be forfeiting many benefits.**

Statutory sick pay (SSP)

Providing you have been paying national insurance contributions, and have been employed for at least eight weeks, the parents will be required to pay you statutory sick pay in accordance with Government legislation if you have been absent from work through ill-health for at least three consecutive days either as part of or instead of your normal pay. This money is recoverable from the Government through the Contributions Agency. For free and confidential advice about Social Security and National Insurance telephone Freeline 0800 666 555.

Maternity rights

If you become pregnant, you are entitled to time off work for antenatal care. If you have been working for six months prior to a date fifteen weeks before your baby is due, the family are required by law to calculate and pay statutory maternity pay, which can be reclaimed in full from the Inland Revenue. This is paid at nine-tenths of your average gross salary for the first six weeks of maternity leave, and then at a fixed rate for a further twelve weeks.

Women have protection against dismissal on grounds of pregnancy even if the employer has written a disclaimer in the original contract. You are entitled to return to work on the same terms as you were employed before. There is no automatic right for a nanny to return to work with her baby. It would be sensible to seek advice from someone qualified in employment law or from the agency, if you should find yourself in a difficult position.

The rules governing statutory maternity pay are complex, and for more information see leaflets FB 8 (*Babies and benefits*) NI 17A (*A detailed guide*) and PL 958 (*Maternity rights*), all available from the benefits agency and local job centres. The Maternity Alliance also offers help. Their address is 35 Beech Street, London, EC2P 2LX. Telephone: 020 7588 8582

Pensions

Pensions are a method of saving for retirement. By law, every working person in the UK has pension provision of some type. If you are not receiving a pension from your employer, and are not self-employed you will receive the basic state pension on reaching retirement age.

As a nanny, you would be unlikely to be offered a pension scheme as you would only expect to work in each job for a limited period of time. Under the government reform of the welfare state, stakeholder pensions were introduced in April 2001, designed for people earning between £9000 and £20,000 pounds a year who do not have access to a better option, such as an occupational pension. These pensions are designed to encourage people to save some of their salary to provide a better quality of life on retirement. The advantage for nannies will be the possibility of moving the pension from employment to employment. A guide to pension options can be obtained by telephoning 0845 731 3233.

Insurance

Your employer will need to hold employer's liability insurance. This will protect them against any legal liabilities incurring as a result of accidental bodily injury to any person working for them during working hours, both on and off the premises. It will also protect them against being sued by you if you should suffer from a serious illness contracted during the course of work.

You need to make sure that you hold personal liability insurance. If you should have an accident while caring for the children either at home or on any outing, and cause them injury or damage your employer's property in a substantial way, you would be able to recover any costs from your insurance. The Professional Association of Nursery Nurses provides this cover for qualified nannies in their membership at no extra charge. Nannies over the age of 19, providing they are studying for an NVQ and have two years' childcare experience and written references are able to purchase through PANN personal liability cover.

Car insurance and use of the car

You will have discussed at interview whether you are allowed or expected to use the family car. It is the responsibility of the employer to ensure that the correct

insurance cover is provided. It is sensible to get permission in writing for you to use the car. The employer should meet any costs attached to your use, unless there are costs due to your professional negligence. For example, you may neglect to put the child in a car seat, and an injury occurs. Therefore, you need to make sure that you have your own liability insurance.

You need to be clear about arrangements made for you to drive the car when you are off duty, and about payments for the petrol. If you are contributing the use of your car, the insurance cover must be fully comprehensive, and you must ensure that you are covered for business use; that is, transporting children. Your employer should pay you a mileage allowance along with any additional agreed sum for the extra insurance, depreciation and car tax, if it is a requirement of the employment that you use your own car.

Young children must always be secured safely in cars, whether it is your car or your employer's. It is your professional responsibility to see that car seats are age and weight appropriate and securely installed. If you have any anxieties about the safety of the equipment, you should refuse to drive the children until any problems have been resolved.

When using a broker to arrange any type of pension or insurance, check that they are registered with Financial Intermediaries, Managers and Brokers Regulatory Authority (FIMBRA), Hertsmere House, Hertsmere Road, London, E14 4AB (telephone: 020 7538 8860).

Budgeting

As a nanny, you may be entrusted regularly with sums of money to cover day-to-day expenses, and for the purchasing of food, clothing or equipment for the children. It is important to keep accurate records of what you receive and what you spend and to meet once a week to discuss the accounts and decide on future spending.

Ask for and keep receipts whenever possible. It is better to discuss the buying of large items first with your employer, bringing home brochures and estimated amounts. Keeping a record will help you keep a check on money coming in and going out (see page 176).

CASE STUDY

Cath started her first nanny job with a family in Derbyshire. She was enjoying her job and getting on well with the parents and the children. There was just one problem. She was continually laying out money for petrol, entrance tickets and swimming and had to ask the parents each time for the money back. This was not always immediately forthcoming, and Cath felt embarrassed to ask again.

1 How might Cath approach this problem with the parents?
2 How might she have avoided the situation?
3 Why might the parents be behaving in this way?

Before agreeing to handle money, be clear about the procedures laid down by your employer. Ensure that you:
- get a receipt for any money, which you pay out, having first ascertained that you have the authority to commit money from your budget. Keep the receipts safe to hand to your employer
- record any payments as soon as possible
- keep a separate purse to hold money and cards belonging to your employer.

Weekly accounts Week beginning:	Mon	Tues	Wed	Thurs	Fri	Sat	Sun
Food							
Chemist							
Pre-school							
School							
Petrol							
Travel							
Clothing							
Newsagent							
Entrance money							
Equipment							
Classes							
Eating out							
Presents for parties							
Books, toys, games							
Other							
Income							
Total in							
Total out							

15 HOW TO WORK IN PARTNERSHIP WITH YOUR FAMILY

> **This chapter includes:**
> - **The parent as the child's main carer**
> - **Understanding various cultures and child-rearing practices**
> - **Your relationship with your employer**
> - **Families under stress**
> - **Confidentiality**
> - **Potential problems**
> - **Dismissal procedure**
> - **Leaving your job**

Once you have decided to embark on a career as a nanny, you will soon realise how important it is to build good relationships with the parents of the children in your care, always keeping in mind that parents are the experts on their own children and respecting their values and opinions. Your relationship with the family will extend to grandparents or other relatives in frequent touch with the family.

Some of the children you care for may be from a background different from your own so you will need to develop a sound understanding of various cultures and child-rearing practices to be able to communicate with the family on a professional level.

Eventually the time will come when you feel it is right for you to move on. The children may all be at school, the family may be moving abroad or you may feel you want to gain new qualifications or work in a different area of childcare. This is often an emotional and difficult time for you and the family because of the close relationships you have formed, but very often nannies remain in touch with the children for many years after leaving.

The parent as the child's main carer

Children will benefit most when the triangle of parent, child and nanny are all working together in harmony.

Parents will know their child's strengths and weaknesses, anticipate their needs and will have made many decisions about their child before employing you. Therefore, it is sensible to work with the parents in all aspects of care and education for the benefit of the child. It will add to the security of the child to see parents and nanny working together and in regular communication.

With any professional relationship, there will be a certain amount of tension and anxiety felt by both yourself and the parents when you first have sole charge of the child.

The parents' range of emotions may include:

- guilt at leaving their child
- anxiety about the safety of the child
- feeling that not knowing enough about childcare and education may impede judging the suitability of the nanny
- doubts about the decision to return to work
- unhappy at the thought of parting from the child
- being upset at possibly missing out on certain milestones, such as finding the first tooth, seeing the first steps and hearing the first words
- anxiety that the nanny will replace them in the child's affections
- worrying that a third adult living in the home might cause difficulties in the parents' relationship
- being able to cope with the logistics of running a home, doing a job, and developing a relationship with the nanny
- worrying how they will manage if the arrangement breaks down.

The nanny's range of emotions may include:
- images of the parents as professional working people, and herself in a lower status job
- fear that she will not be able to form a satisfactory relationship with the parents
- fear that she may not like the child
- worries about cultural and social differences
- worries that her knowledge and skills are sufficient to equip her to do the job satisfactorily.

The parents may give you a great deal of information about the children. Equally you may find that they are new inexperienced parents, who are not sure what you need to know. In addition to the chart on pages 30–31, 'Care needs', you may find the following information helpful:
- the names of other members of the child's family
- the names and habits of pets
- special words and names and other vocabulary used by the child
- anything the child finds alarming or unsettling, perhaps dogs, people in spectacles, or beards
- whether the child can use a cup and what eating implements she uses
- whether the child still has a nap and if there are any routines which help the child to sleep
- whether there is anyone who is not permitted contact with the child
- any new factors or special problems in the child's life.

Understanding various cultures and child-rearing practices

Children are brought up in many different types of families including:
- the nuclear family, which is a small family unit of parents and children with no other family members living with them
- the extended family, which includes parents, children, and other family members who may live with the family or close by, and who are in frequent contact with each other
- the lone-parent family, sometimes known as the single- or one-parent family, comprising the mother or the father plus their children. Roughly 90 per cent of these households are headed by the mother and 10 per cent by the father. Of the women, about 60 per cent are divorced or separated, 23 per cent are single and 7 per cent widowed
- the reconstituted family, sometimes known as the 'blended' family, where parents have divorced or separated and remarried or are living with new partners and perhaps their children
- a homosexual partnership where two men or two women are living together with the children of a previous heterosexual partnership, or in some gay relationships, their own children. All the research carried out since the sixties

shows no differences in the social and emotional development of children living in these households, or to their gender orientation.

You may find yourself working for any of the types of family described above. It is hoped that you would know this at interview, as this might form part of your decision making. For example, you might find it challenging to work with a reconstituted family where there could be tensions in the parents' relationships.

CASE STUDY

Vanessa lives in with a family of three children, including a baby, the parents and the mother's mother. Granny creates all kinds of problems when the parents are out at work. She overrules Vanessa's decisions, smokes in front of the children, disrupts the daily routine and constantly criticises Vanessa's skills and knowledge.

1   How might Vanessa tackle this problem?
2   Should she speak to the parents about it?
3   How might the parents react?

After a while, you will start to feel part of the family, and you should be made to feel comfortable with close relatives, and accepted by them. From the start, you need to talk to your employers about their families so that you know who everyone is and have some idea of how they relate to one another, and in particular to the children. If grandparents live close by, you may well see them during the day without the parents being present, and will soon appreciate how much they have to offer.

Nannies should provide care that is consistent with that of the parents. Children's needs and parents wishes may derive from a cultural or religious source, or from medical reasons, or quite simply, that is what the parents want for their child. Parents' wishes and child-rearing practices must be respected and every effort made to comply with them.

Nannies and parents should discuss and come to agreements about matters relating to:

- food, its preparation and eating, for example meat free or exclusion of certain meats
- personal hygiene, for example use of toilet and hand-washing
- skin and hair care, for example creams and combs suitable for some African-Caribbean children
- the question of clothing during play, for example, maintaining modesty in physical play, covering very curly or braided hair for sand play, or protecting against strong sunlight
- periods of rest and sleep, for example routines, comfort objects or activities such as massage.

Do not assume that because a family is part of a particular cultural group, they follow all the practices of that culture. It is essential to discuss all aspects of the child's care with the parents and find out how they wish you to care for their child.

CASE STUDY

Cynthia has accepted a post with a Muslim family where she will have sole charge of their three-year-old daughter and eighteen-month-old son.

1   What will Cynthia need to ask the parents?
2   How will she demonstrate to the parents that she can provide the care they wish for their children?
3   What differences in the care of the children might there be?

Once agreement has been reached, respect parents' wishes and stick to the practices agreed. Not to do this would represent a betrayal of parents' trust and demonstrate a lack of respect for their views and childcare practices.

Your relationship with your employer

Living and working in a family home is difficult and there may have to be a great deal of give and take. You having a close relationship with the children may be hard for your employer, and you must be prepared for some ups and downs. Your relationship with your employer is crucial to the success of the arrangement, and, as in any relationship, the key lies in communication.

COMMUNICATING WITH YOUR EMPLOYER

Communications between you and the parents need to be clear and uncomplicated at all times if you are to establish a harmonious partnership. You will need to be able to convey your expectations to them while at the same time listening to their point of view. Lack of communication can lead to misunderstandings and this may affect the children.

It is important to set aside a time either weekly or daily, at which to discuss with your employer any problems that may have occurred, achievements that have been made and any changes that need to be put in place. This may be half an hour at the end of each day to begin with and then reduced to just an hour a week as you settle in. Nevertheless, don't allow this important slot to disappear altogether: the children are growing and developing all the time and you don't want the parents to lose touch with what is going on.

Communication is a two-way process, and efforts will have to be made on both sides. Always be available if your employer rings you. Sharing a daily information chart with your employer, as shown on page 33, is an excellent way of helping you both to keep in touch with the day-to-day events. You could use this as the basis for your daily or weekly update, going through the chart and discussing each child and their activities.

Cherie, a hospital consultant, employed a highly qualified and experienced residential nanny, Greta, to care for her first baby. She was about to return to work and felt confident that Greta would look after her baby exactly as she wished. During the induction week, it became clear that Greta disapproved of her practice of taking the baby into her bed overnight, stating that she was 'making a rod for her own back'.

Cherie understood the point that Greta made, and the next night when the baby cried, tried to comfort him in his own room. When this did not work, she gave in and took the baby into bed with her. In the morning, she quietly and calmly told Greta that this was right for her and her baby, and that she had every confidence that it would not damage the baby, and that he would grow into an independent secure child.

1   Do you think Cherie or Greta was in the right?

2   Why?

Families under stress

The families of the children you care for might be feeling stress for many reasons. This might occur after you have been employed, or be long standing. The parents may become:

- difficult to communicate with
- reluctant to meet their responsibilities towards you, such as being slow to pay you or changing your time off at short notice
- reluctant to discuss the needs of the child
- uninterested in the child's achievements
- depressed and unresponsive to offers of support
- angry and aggressive towards you
- frequently arriving home late.

The stress experienced by the parents might cause the children to:

- be difficult to manage
- be clinging and fretful
- show anxiety at separation from the parents
- display mood swings, ranging from being withdrawn to being aggressive
- show an increase in comfort behaviour
- regress in development
- not look forward to the parents returning home.

A situation in the family where the child is obviously unhappy cannot be left to resolve itself. This is also true if the parents are taking advantage of your good nature and not contributing to a positive working relationship. If you find yourself in this position you will attempt to:

- acknowledge your feelings. Seek opportunities to communicate with the parents in a non-threatening, non-judgemental manner

- be up front and assertive. State your needs to the parents
- keep calm if you have to deal with an angry parent. Listen to what is being said and do not respond in an aggressive way yourself
- keep meticulous records of the child's behaviour and incidents involving the parents
- employ stress-management techniques.

CASE STUDY

Sadie is an experienced nanny, who has been caring for Rosie, aged two years, for the last three months. She has established a good working relationship with Rosie's mother. On at least two occasions, her employer has been home very late, smelling of alcohol and not wishing to spend any time with Rosie.

1 How do you think Sadie should handle this?
2 How can Sadie support and advise her employer?
3 How can Sadie make sure that Rosie still feels loved and secure?

GOOD PRACTICE IN WORKING WITH PARENTS

1 Respect all parents as individuals, and learn from them different ways of child rearing. Their ideas and practices may be different from yours, but are no less valid. Be open to a variety of opinions.
2 Respect parents' values, practices and preferences.
3 Maintain and contribute to a welcoming and relaxed atmosphere in the home.
4 Remember the parents are the experts on their own individual children.
5 Try to communicate, at the end of the day, the important aspects of the child's day, sharing negative and positive situations alike.
6 Be professional at all times. Never gossip about parents to other parents. Refuse to listen to other people's unsubstantiated hearsay.
7 Offer reassurance and encouragement to parents, always emphasising the central role parents play in their children's lives.
8 Do not become over-involved with the children so that you appear to be taking over from the parents.
9 Be clear about the contract and job description. The more time you spend in discussion with the parents during the interview, and perhaps in other discussion prior to accepting the job, the less likelihood there is that there will be problems.

Confidentiality

You would be expected not to gossip about your employer or anyone in the family. In fact, most contracts contain a confidentiality clause stating that a nanny agrees not to discuss or divulge any private matters now, or in the future, unless required to by law. This may apply if the parents have arranged for you to communicate with the school or family doctor, for example. You may well receive confidential information and you would be expected to pass that information on only to your employer.

On a personal level, spending time in the home you may become aware of domestic disagreements, business matters or difficulties with the extended family. Indeed you might find out something that could be potentially damaging to the family. You would only betray this trust if you thought the children were at risk of abuse.

If you are alone in the house, you may see private documents and correspondence left lying around, or receive telephone messages for your employer. It might be a good idea to ask your employer to be more discreet, as you wish to respect their privacy. By doing this, you will be demonstrating that they have selected a nanny who is eminently trustworthy and loyal.

It is hoped that the family will respect your privacy, and would not think of entering your room to read your private correspondence or to check up on your personal affairs.

Potential problems

However happy a relationship you have with the family, an awareness of potential difficulties will help you to avoid them. The most frequent areas of tension are thought to include:

- lack of clarity in the job description
- personality differences
- disagreements about discipline and routines
- lack of sensitivity to your privacy
- differences over your social life
- not being clear as to your relationship with your family: are you a friend or an employee?
- feelings of jealousy about the affection the children feel for you, and the amount of time you are able to spend with them
- conditions of service including salary, time off and perks
- the children disliking you
- you disliking the children
- you having no friends or interests outside the job
- you having too many friends and interests outside the job
- different standards of personal hygiene and general lack of cleanliness in the home
- sexual harrassment by a member of the family or family friend.

If any of these problems occur, in spite of a full and frank interview, a job description and a contract of employment, the best way of dealing with it is to talk about it with the parents as soon as possible, and attempt to reach a solution which is obtainable by both of you. If you feel uncomfortable in tackling an issue, the agency or your union might be able to intercede for you.

Any issue that needs to be discussed with your employer will need some thought on your part first. Spend some time discussing it with a close friend, so

that you are clear about what you hope to achieve. Arrange a time to speak to your employer when there should be few interruptions. Remain calm and never lose your temper. Be ready to compromise and show some flexibility.

The most frequent complaints from nannies about their employers are:

- being asked to work overtime too frequently, without much notice, and at the same rate of pay
- being over-ruled in disciplinary matters
- not being given a full and honest job description
- low pay
- not being consulted about holiday dates, or other changes to the routine in good time
- having their private life interfered with and being offered unwanted advice
- not having agreed consistency in the care of the child
- automatically being blamed for any problem
- not being allowed to have their boyfriends to stay
- not having enough to eat
- not being shown appreciation or gratitude.

If you attempt to ignore an area of conflict between yourself and one or both of the parents, the children will sense the atmosphere and may become distressed. Older children may attempt to manipulate the situation.

Sometimes, due to a personality clash, or to inflexible rigid ideas, it is impossible to come to an agreement and, for the sake of the children, you may decide to leave. This rarely happens, if enough time and effort have been put into the interviewing and selection process.

Dismissal procedure

If the worst comes to the worst and you find that for some reason your employer decides to terminate your employment, you need to know the correct procedure for dismissal.

The terms of dismissal will be clearly stated in your contract. By law, if you have worked at least one month but less than two years service you must receive a minimum of one week's notice. Thereafter, you are entitled to be given at least one week's notice for each complete year of service up to twelve weeks. The notice required by law from you is one week after one month's continuous service, and the minimum does not increase with the length of employment. These provisions apply to all terminations of employment, except on ground of summary dismissal (dismissed on the spot). Reasons giving rise to summary dismissal include:

- theft
- alcohol abuse
- illegal drug taking
- child abuse.

The employment may also be terminated if:

- you are incompetent or unqualified to do the job
- your professional conduct is unacceptable, or
- your post becomes redundant for some reason.

The contract of employment should be terminated by your employer in writing, stating the reasons clearly, indicating the period of notice and including details of any payments due. If you resign, you should give formal notice in writing as stated in the contract. Employment law is complicated and if a dispute threatens to arise it may be wise to seek professional advice from your union or a solicitor.

In general, employers should tackle issues that they find annoying as soon as possible. For example, if your employer is unhappy with your hygiene when preparing food, she must speak to you about this and indicate the standard she expects. If no discussion takes place, the employer is laying herself open to a charge of unfair dismissal, as you can justly say that you never received a verbal warning, and you had no idea that you were doing anything wrong until you were suddenly dismissed. A claim for unfair dismissal can be heard by an employment tribunal.

Leaving your job

When the time has come to leave, you will need to plan with your employer how to make this break, causing as little upset as possible to the children. Tell them honestly what is happening, and try to give them as much time as you can to get them accustomed to the situation. Reassure them that you will keep in touch and visit them if this is at all possible. It may be possible to get a new nanny in post before you leave, and the children and the new nanny will all benefit from a short handing-over period.

APPENDIX

Nanny Contract of Employment

Date of Issue:...

Name and Address of Employer:..

....

....

Name and Address of Employee: ....

....

....

Date of Commencement of Employment: ....

Job Title: ....

REMUNERATION

The salary is . . . . per *week/month *before/after deduction of Tax and National

Insurance payable on . . . .

The employer will be responsible for accounting for the employer's and employee's National Insurance Contributions and Income Tax.

The employer will ensure that the employee is given a payslip on the day of payment detailing gross payment, deductions and net payment.

The salary will be reviewed *once/twice per year on . . . .

Length of probationary period . . . .

NOTES FOR INFORMATION

> **Hours of Work**
>
> *Employment in a private household is such that it is difficult to define exact hours of work and free time. While it is difficult to set exact hours, PANN encourages good employment practices; carers should not be expected to work unreasonable hours.*

(*Delete where applicable)

Normal hours of work will be from. . . . . am to . . . . pm daily. It is intended you will,

however, have. . . . . free days per week and/or . . . . free weekends per month,

from . . . . (time / day) to . . . . (time / day).

These arrangements can only be changed by mutual consent.

Notes for Information

> *Occasional overnight care - prior arrangement - may be needed, for which extra payment will be made. (Usually paid at the rate of babysitting fee, from the end of normal working day up to midnight). You must agree a maximum number of hours to be worked per week. Babysitting requirements should be stipulated in the contract with a minimum of 24 hours' notice required, unless in an emergency. Babysitting twice a week would be considered reasonable, anything extra, such as Sundays and the occasional overnight duty if required, should attract additional reward.*

HOLIDAYS

You will be allowed . . . . weeks' paid holiday in each year. In the first or final year of service the employee will be entitled to holidays on a pro rata basis.

Notes for Information

> *Nannies should be awarded at least four weeks' annual holiday plus bank holidays. Holidays taken with the family are **not** to be considered as part of your nanny's annual leave. Any statutory bank holidays worked **should** be paid at double time or double time off in lieu.*
>
> *Your nanny should be paid in your absence, for example, if you go away on holiday and do not wish her to join you, she remains in your employ. Also, if you are going to be away for some time, your nanny should be paid a retainer.*
>
> *Paid compensation is not normally given for holidays not actually taken. Holidays may only be carried into the next year with the express permission of the employer.*

Child's/Children's ages: . . . .

The employee shall be entitled to:

a)   Accommodation: . . . .

b)   Bathroom *sole use/shared: . . . .

c)   Meals (please specify): . . . .

d)   Use of car *on duty/off duty: . . . .

   Petrol costs will be reimbursed at the rate recommended by the AA if the employee uses his/her own car.

e)   Other benefits: . . . .
(*Delete where applicable)

SICKNESS

The employer will administer the Government SSP scheme in accordance with legislation.

After 8 weeks of employment, the employer will pay the employee full pay for a period of . . . . .weeks,

then . . . . pay for . . . . weeks.

After that period, SSP only will be due.

TERMINATION

In the first 4 weeks' of employment, one week's notice is required on either side.

After four weeks' continuous service, either the employee or the employer may terminate this contract by

giving . . . . weeks' notice.

CONFIDENTIALITY

It is a condition of employment that now and at all times in the future, save as may be lawfully required, the employee shall keep the affairs and concerns of the householder and its transactions and business confidential.

PENSIONS

The employer *does/does not run a pension scheme.

NOTES FOR INFORMATION

> For further information, see Royal National Pension Fund for Nurses under Further Information Section.

DISCIPLINE

Reasons which might give rise to the need for disciplinary measures include the following:

a) Causing a disruptive influence in the household
b) Job incompetence
c) Unsatisfactory standard of dress or appearance
d) Conduct during or outside working hours prejudicial to the interest or reputation of the employer
e) Unreliability in time keeping or attendance
f) Failure to comply with instructions and procedures, for example being unable to drive due to driving ban
g) Breach of confidentiality clause

(*Delete where applicable)

In the event of the need to take disciplinary action, the procedure will be:

Firstly   -   Oral warning
Secondly -   Written warning
Thirdly   -   Dismissal

The nanny should have the right to appeal to an agreed third party. (See Grievances below.)

Reasons which might give rise to summary dismissal include the following:

a)   Child abuse
b)   Drunkenness
c)   Illegal drug taking
d)   Theft

GRIEVANCES

If the employee has any grievance against the employer, she has the right to seek advice (for example from PANN, family solicitor, nanny agencies, etc).

NOTES FOR INFORMATION

MISCELLANEOUS

Nannies are advised to have written details of insurance policies in place and written authority covering taking children to participate in sporting activities, such as swimming. They should also have written permission covering emergency procedures, for example authority to act in the parent(s)' absence. If in doubt, please contact PANN for advice.

....
Signed by the employer

....
Signed by the employee

Date . . . .

FURTHER READING

Babies

Dare, A. and O'Donovan, M., *A Practical Guide to Working with Babies*, 2nd edition, Stanley Thornes, 1998

Goldschmied, E. and Jackson, S., *People Under Three,* Routledge, 1994

Hollyer, B. and Smith, L., *Sleep: the Secret of Problem Free Nights,* Ward Lock, 1996

Leach, P., *Babyhood*, Penguin, 1991

Sheridan, M., *From Birth to Five Years* (revised and updated by Frost, M. and Sharma, A.), Routledge, 1997

Valman, H.B., *The First Year of Life,* 4th edition, BMJ Publishing Group, 1995

Disability

ACE Special Education Handbook, *The Law on Children with Special Needs*, ACE, 1996

Dare, A. and O'Donovan, M., *Good Practice in Caring for Young Children with Special Needs*, Stanley Thornes, 1997

Play and learning

Best Guide to Days Out Ever, Best Guides Ltd, 1997

Bright Ideas for Early Years Series and *Bright Ideas Series,* Scholastic Publications Ltd

Butler, D., *Babies Need Books*, 3rd edition, Penguin, 1995

Hobart, C. and Frankel, J., *A Practical Guide to Activities for Young Children*, 2nd edition, Stanley Thornes, 1999

Communication

Crystal, D., *Listen to Your Child*, Penguin, 1986

Hobart, C. and Frankel, J., *A Practical Guide to Child Observation and Assessment*, 2nd edition, Stanley Thornes, 1999

Mukherji, P. and O'Dea, T., *Understanding Children's Language and Literacy*, Stanley Thornes, 2000

Petrie, P., *Communication with Children and Adults*, Edward Arnold, 1989

Ward, S., *Baby Talk,* Century, 2000

Behaviour

Einon, D., *Child Behaviour*, Viking (Penguin), 1997
Mukherji, P., *Understanding Children's Challenging Behaviour*, Nelson Thornes, 2001
Richman, N. and Lansdown, R. (eds), *Problems of Pre-school Children*, John Wiley & Sons, 1988

Nutrition

Dare, A. and O'Donovan, M., *A Practical Guide to Child Nutrition*, Stanley Thornes, 1996
Hollyer, B. and Smith, L., *Feeding: The Simple Solution*, Ward Lock, 1997
Whiting, M. and Lobstein, T., *The Nursery Food Book*, Edward Arnold, 1992

Safety and First Aid

Elliot, M., *Keeping Safe: A Practical Guide to Talking to Children*, Coronet, 1994
First Aid for Children – Fast, Dorling Kindersley with the British Red Cross, 1994
Dare, A. and O'Donovon, M., *Good Practice in Child Safety*, Nelson Thornes, 2000
Hobart, C. and Frankel, J., *Good Practice in Child Protection*, Stanley Thornes, 1998
Levene, S., *Play It Safe: The Complete Guide to Child Accident Prevention*, BBC Books, 1992
Wolfe, L., *Safe and Sound*, Hodder & Stoughton, 1993

Health

Brown, H. (ed.), *Which Guide to Child Health*, Which Books, 1997
Gilbert, P., *The A-Z Reference Book of Childhood Conditions*, Chapman & Hall, 1995
Keene, A., *Child Health, Care of the Child in Health and Illness*, Stanley Thornes, 1999
Stoppard, M., *Complete Baby and Childcare*, Dorling Kindersley, 1995

USEFUL CONTACTS

Best Guides Ltd
PO Box 427, Northampton NN2 7YJ
Telephone: 01604 711 994

Council for Disabled Children
Telephone: 020 7843 6000

Galt Toys
Brookfield Road, Cheadle, Cheshire SK8 2PN
Telephone: 0161 428 9111 (toy catalogue)

Nanny Tax
PO Box 988, Brighton BN2 1BY
Telephone: 01273 626 256

National Children's Bureau
8 Wakely Street, London EC1V 7QE

Nursery World and Professional Nanny
Lector Court, 151/153 Farringdon Road, London EC1R 3AD
Telephone: 020 7837 7224

Professional Association of Nursery Nurses (PANN)
2 St James's Court, Friar Gate, Derby DE1 1BT
Telephone: 01332 372 337

Recruitment and Employment Federation
36 Mortimer Street, London W1N 7RB
Telephone: 020 7323 4300

Scholastic Publications Ltd
Freepost CV 1034, Westfield Road, Southern Leamington Spa
Warwickshire CV33 0BR

St John Ambulance
Telephone: 020 7235 5231

INDEX

Page references in italics indicate tables or figures.

dental hygiene 45
encouraging personal hygiene 46
food 51–4, *53*
prevention of infection 70, 82–3
skin and hair care 42–3

illness
caring for unwell children 79–81
chronic medical conditions 90–3
infection 81–3
infestations 89
minor ailments 83–7, *83*, *86*
minor illness escalating 87–8
recognition of 77–9, *78*
school-age children 157
imaginary play 115–16
impetigo *86*
income tax 171–2
infection 69, 81–2
common childhood infections *78*
minor ailments 84
preventing cross-infection 82–3
prevention 70
prevention in babies 138
infestations 89
insurance 173
intellectual development
pre-school children 149
school-age children 153
toddlers 146–7
interviews, job
body language 21
the interview 18–20
preparation 17–18
isolation 38

jaundice *88*
jealousy 125
jigsaw puzzles 117
job description 24–5
job search 12
accepting the job 21–2
agencies 12–13
answering individual advertisements 13–14
curriculum vitae (CV) 15–17

interview preparation 17–18
interviews 18–21
job applications 15, *16*
professional journals and newspapers 14–15
telephone technique 17
see also employment

language development
developing children's skills 97–9
pre-school children 149
school-age children 153
toddlers 146–7
Lean on Me (support group) 38
learning 110
early years curriculum 150–1
see also development; play
lice 89
listening skills
communicating with adults 100
developing children's 99
listeria 53
local environment 36–7
lone-parent families 179
loneliness 38

manipulative skills 99
activities that aid 118
pre-school children 149
school-age children 153
toddlers 145–6
masturbation 132
matching games 118
maternity rights 172–3
mealtimes
causing conflict 130–1
eating patterns 54–6
encouraging children to eat *55*
encouraging healthy eating habits 56
reasons for food refusal *55*
see also nutrition
measles *78*, *86*
medical information *35*
medication 71
administering 80